The Official 2016 Annual

In loving memory of our dear colleague Neale Pirie: 1973-2015

Alison Maloney

BOOKS

CONTENTS

Tess Daly

Strictly's very own Belle of the Ballroom is back where she belongs for the new series and raring to go. She's been casting her expert eye over the latest batch of nervous novices and she likes what she sees.

'It's an interesting mixture of people,' she says. 'We've got well-known personalities such as Peter Andre, whom, I'm sure will be a hit with the ladies. We have current-affairs broadcasters such as Jeremy Vine, who is really up for the crack, and we have a huge, bubbly personality in Ainsley Harriott. He's so excited I just want to cuddle him.

'Olympian Iwan Thomas is like a giddy kitten. He can't stay still; he's prancing up and down on the spot. He loves the Lycra and the sequins, but he can't wait to take it all off. He might be first for the topless paso.

'We have our gorgeous ladies too. Jamelia certainly looks the part and wants to impress her daughters. Kirsty Gallacher is athletic, strong and trains every day. She's got some guns on her. Anita Rani is petite, beautiful and competitive, and she was hilarious when she was paired with Gleb Savchenko. She was so intimated by his beauty she couldn't make eye contact.'

As our *Strictly* spy, Tess had a sneaky peak at the snake-hipped celebs in rehearsals, and she thinks there's some serious girl power heading to the dance floor.

'The girls are strong this year. Helen George has a fluidity to her movement that spells great potential, so she's one to watch. Georgia May Foote is beautiful, and the little girls at home will love her because she looks like a Disney princess.

Our new dancer Giovanni Pernice thought all his Christmases had come at once when he landed her.

'Carol Kirkwood has sunshine in her smile and lights up the room. She is gorgeous but she's definitely the most terrified.'

But Tess has also spotted some hot potential among the boys.

'Peter is going to wow us all,' she predicts. 'Watching the group rehearsal, I caught a glimpse of Peter from behind and for a moment I thought it was Giovanni! He was so good he took my breath away.

'Boxer Anthony Ogogo is a gorgeous-looking chap but nursing an injury so he was very reluctant to use that arm. He's light on his feet, used to dancing round the ring in boxing, but he's actually a pussycat and very shy.

'I had a lot of shy boys on my hands at the launch show. Jay McGuiness was quaking in his dancing shoes, which is incredible considering he has performed in front of thousands on arena tours. When I watched him in training, he was dancing on the tip of his toes, on the balls of his feet, and he looked like he could be really good. But he needs to find his confidence.'

The most shocking moment of the launch, for Tess, was Katie Derham's pairing with Anton Du Beke. In his 12 years on the show, the seasoned pro has never made it to the final. Maybe this time …

'I've never seen Anton speechless and he almost was. Katie is incredibly elegant. She has a beautiful balletic poise and she's so graceful in the way she moves. Let's not forget Anton has never had a ten, so Katie could be the girl who takes him there. I hope so.'

Claudia Winkleman

Presenting *Strictly Come Dancing* was a dream come true for Claudia, not least because she got to front the show with Tess Daly. Saturday night's latest double act have been friends for years and Claudia can't wait to team up again.

'I had the best time last year,' she reveals. 'I love Tess so much, and we laughed a lot. I hope I did a good job because I absolutely loved it, and I am thrilled to be back again.'

It's not just her co-presenter or the glamour of the glittery frocks that has Claudia excited. After years of fronting *It Takes Two*, the kooky presenter is still bowled over by the dancers.

'Yesterday I was at rehearsals and I watched the pros do a dance,' she says. 'I get real goosebumps. The hairs on the back of my neck actually stand up, and I think I've got the best job in the world.'

Even so, the queen of the Clauditorium – as Tess's balcony area has now been dubbed – admits to some nerves.

'I'm still completely terrified as well as being incredibly excited,' she confesses. '*Strictly* is by far the biggest thing I've ever done, so I'm always worried that I'm going to mess up, that I'm going to fall over, that I'm going to be too orange, that I'm going to ask something stupid, so I'm completely jumpy and nervous.'

Her favourite moment of the last series was the showdance that clinched the title for Caroline Flack and Pasha Kovalev, and 'made everyone cry'. But she says what struck her most was the atmosphere backstage.

'The camaraderie among all the dancers was fantastic. They were really fun, they had a great time together and they were all so friendly.'

But having eyed up the latest batch of hopefuls, Claudia reckons we are in for another treat.

'The line-up is fantastic,' she says. 'They're really funny and they've all just thrown themselves in. In rehearsals for the launch show Jeremy and Ainsley were just like, Wow. We're dancing! They were so chuffed. There was no one saying, "I don't want to wear anything tight" or "Please can I wear no pink?" They were all fully immersed from day one.'

The Strictlification of the celebs is all part of the process, and when the spray tans have dried and the sequins are glistening in the studio lights, Claudia is in her element.

'I cannot wait, because once they've got their clothes on it all becomes real,' she says. 'Georgia May Foote is singly the most beautiful creature I have ever met, so she will look gorgeous, and Jamelia will look amazing. But all of them will. That's the beauty of *Strictly*.'

Despite being part of the *Strictly* family, one way or another, for a decade, Claudia admits she's 'terrible at dancing' and not much better at picking a potential winner.

'I think that Katie Derham might be amazing,' she muses. 'But I'm always rubbish at guessing who might win and I predict very badly. So whatever I say is likely to be wrong!'

FABULOUS FLACK

Strictly champ Caroline Flack may have bagged three perfect scores in the series 12 final, but being handed the glitterball trophy still came as a shock. In fact, the TV presenter thought she was having a *Zoolander* moment.

'It took ages to sink in,' she laughs. 'It didn't feel real at all. You know that famous scene in *Zoolander*, when he gets up to pick up an award and his name hasn't been called? I was thinking, Oh my God, did they call my name or have I just celebrated because I thought they called my name? It was a real shock. We'd had a great final, we got brilliant scores and we had a brilliant time, but we didn't expect to win at all.'

The Norfolk-born star, who admits she has wanted to be on the show since it first began, was thrilled to be paired with Pasha Kovalev on the launch show.

'I liked Pasha instantly,' she reveals. 'They introduce you to all the dancers at the same time, and it's a bit like speed-dating, because you go round and talk to everybody. Everything about Pasha told me he would make the perfect partner for me.'

But just because the pair quickly became friends off the floor doesn't mean the Russian tutor gave his pupil an easy ride in the rehearsal room.

'Pasha is very thorough and quite strict,' she reveals. 'He's very serious in rehearsals and I like to mess around quite a lot, but he would say, "Get back to work!" In training, he goes into dance-teacher mode – but I needed that.'

What Flack lacked in discipline, however, she made up for in enthusiasm. Having taken on the *Strictly* challenge, she cleared her diary and threw herself into training.

'I wanted to go in every day, early morning, and we didn't finish until late, so I literally gave up everything to do it. I just wanted to focus on this, and I really enjoyed the rehearsals.

'I was very lucky I didn't have to do another job, like Jake Wood. Our rehearsals were quite relaxed in that sense, so we could have an hour's lunch and stop for a coffee when we needed to. We had a great time.'

The pair kicked off the series with their cha-cha-cha, but there were no first-night nerves.

'In a way being first made it easier because I didn't have time to get nervous,' she says. 'In fact, it was my favourite performance because I didn't know what to expect, I didn't know how it would feel, and the audience were so behind us. It's the first time in my whole life I've done anything like that, so it was amazing.

'I got more nervous as the weeks went on, the pressure was on and we knew what to expect. The further you get, the more you want to stay.'

While Caroline's Latin had the judges reaching for the high numbers, she struggled with the ballroom dances and found the positioning of the head and arms difficult to perfect. Her bid for the glitterball suffered a blow at the halfway mark, when she ended up in the dance-off with her waltz.

'Being in the bottom two is horrible, but it's when you go to rehearsal on the Monday morning that it feels the worst,' she explains. 'I felt like I'd let Pasha down, and I spent the next few days in tears. Pasha was like, "Stop crying!"'

The couple's luck changed the following week, when their Argentine tango caused Bruno to utter Caroline's favourite comment of the series: 'If you were a violin, you would be a Stradivarius.' But it was the final that showed how far the star had come, and her romantic barefoot showdance, to Robbie Williams's 'Angels', had the nation enthralled and went down in the annals of *Strictly* history as an all-time classic.

'That was my favourite dance,' she reveals.

'I loved the idea of it. I also loved kicking off the dancing shoes because I really struggled in those heels.'

Caroline admits she was initially wary of the swathes of silk that billowed from her waist, blown by wind machines, at the start of the routine.

'In rehearsal we just had little electric fans all over the studio,' she says. 'I said to Pasha, "This is never going to work!", and he said, "Trust me, it will work." It took so much rehearsing, because I had Velcro round my waist and they were attached to that, and Pasha had to undo the Velcro and chuck the belt away without anybody seeing.'

The stunning showdance, the centrepiece of the couple's perfect final, was also the most moving dance for the would-be champ.

'It was the most difficult routine, but there was something about it that made it really emotional,' she recalls. 'I didn't realise I was so emotional but it expressed everything that Pasha and I had been through in the whole series. I loved it.'

Caroline's 'phenomenal' Charleston to 'Istanbul (Not Constantinople)' was no turkey.

'I didn't realise I was so emotional, but it expressed everything that Pasha and I had been through in the whole series. I loved it.'

By the time she floated across the floor in her semi-final foxtrot to 'Diamonds', Caroline was a polished gem.

Caroline's debut cha-cha-cha had Darcey telling her she was a 'natural dancer'. Not a bad start.

THE JUDGES ON CAROLINE

Len on the jive:
'The jive is all about kicks and flicks. You can't half flick, Flack.'

• • •

Bruno on the Charleston:
'That was like the Orient Express. Beautiful to look at, perfect in every detail and a ride you'll never forget.'

• • •

Craig on the Charleston:
'My heart has melted. You are phenomenal.'

• • •

Darcey on the showdance:
'It was like watching a beautiful contemporary ballet. You'd be in my company any day.'

• • •

Len on the showdance:
'You didn't need wind machines. You've got huge fans up here.'

Len Goodman

Head judge Len has been polishing up his metaphors and dusting off his famous 'Se-ven' paddle for this year's *Strictly Come Dancing*. And after two years of dancing queens he's hoping the new series can throw up a king.

'We haven't had a male champ since Louis Smith in 2012 so it would be nice to see one of the boys win it,' he admits. 'But the girls are looking very strong this year. Girls generally are better at dancing because most little girls go to ballet schools or other dance classes while the boys are playing football.

'Then again who would have thought that Mark Wright, who had never danced in his life, would make it into the final four last year? There are surprises in every series and that's the fascination of the show.'

What do you make of the line-up?
I like it. We've got so many walks of life. We have a boxer, singers, a chef, journalists and presenters, an athlete, a weather girl plus somebody from both *EastEnders* and *Coronation Street*. There are a few people in their fifties, which is great, and there's no obvious John Sergeant comedy person to act as cannon fodder for Craig.

Who would you predict for the finals?
It's difficult having only seen the group dance but I'd have to go with Georgia May Foote, especially with a name like Foote. She should be good on her feet. I like the look of Katie Derham. Could this be the year that Anton makes the final? Peter Andre must be in for a shot, but my outsider would be

Ainsley Harriot. On *Ready Steady Cook*, he always put plenty of wiggle in, plus he has a wonderful personality.

What do you make of the sportsmen?
Anthony Ogogo could be a contender, but boxers have always been terrible on *Strictly*. You'd think they'd be light on their feet but in the US we had two of the greatest boxers of all time, Sugar Ray Leonard and Floyd Mayweather Jr., and here we had Joe Calzaghe and Audley Harrison; none of theme was much cop. But cricketers and rugby players, who you wouldn't expect to be able to dance, are often really good. Iwan Thomas is fit and he'll have that competitive edge, but he doesn't look like a dancer to me. An old dance teacher once told me, "The best dancer doesn't always win. It's the one who *looks* the best dancer." There is a difference.

Who will the public back?
The public love Ainsley Harriott. He's a very popular guy. Daniel O'Donnell is the Irish Elvis, so if his massive fan base get behind him, he could stay. Carol is very popular too. A lot of my mates from the golf club have a real soft spot for her!

Was Caroline Flack a deserving champ?
When it came down to the final three last year, they were all deserving. But Caroline danced on the launch show this year and she was fabulous. All the new celebrities must have been watching it, thinking, Blimey, that's the standard I've got to get to. Terrifying.

Katie Derham

Broadcaster Katie knew just where to turn for advice after signing up for the show. Even before she started training with Anton du Beke, she'd been getting a head start with 15-year-old daughter Natasha.

'Both my girls think it's tremendous that I'm doing the show,' she says. 'Natasha is a keen dancer and she's been putting me through my paces at home, but I can't do anything she can do. She's really good. She can put her leg up to her ear!

'She told me I had to improve my core and work on the fouetté. I mean, what *is* a fouetté? I have no idea. She's really thrilled for me but there's quite a lot of pressure not to let her and her dancing friends down. My 10-year-old, Eleanor, just wants to see all the wonderful costumes.'

The BBC broadcaster has worn her fair share of posh frocks, having fronted coverage of the Proms for the last five years, but she is still loving the glamour of the *Strictly* sequins.

'We don't look like us at all when we're dressed up but you have to embrace the *Strictly* world,' she says. 'I'm a huge fan and always have been. It's a very positive, fun show, it looks great, it's a fun fantasy and we're really lucky to be in it. It is lovely getting into those fabulous frocks. You put them on and you feel good.'

Even before she danced a step, Katie was getting into the *Strictly* sparkle – literally.

'Our first day of filming I had the classic direction: "Now, Katie, can you just show us a few moves for 30 seconds while we fire glitter at you?" Never did I think I'd get that direction in my life!'

The 45-year-old presenter is the perfect pairing for ballroom king Anton, as her favourite dance is the American smooth. 'I love the music, the American-songbook style, Sinatra and Cole Porter,' she says. 'That will be the one I most want to dance.'

But she admits she is worried by the possibility of making a blunder.

'Having seen the size of the dance floor,' she laughs. 'I do suspect I'll end up in somebody's lap.'

Anton Du Beke

With former celeb partners Ann Widdecombe, Nancy Dell'Olio and last year's Judy Murray, waltzing wag Anton has provided some of the most memorable moments of *Strictly*'s history. But this year he's set to get serious, with BBC presenter Katie Derham.

'She's amazing and dead keen, and that's the lovely thing. She's been a mega-fan of *Strictly* for 12 series so it's like a dream come true, for both of us. And she gets to dance with me – what could be better!'

Despite being the longest-serving professional, along with Brendan Cole, Anton has never made it to the final and never got a ten. He's hoping Katie will be the girl who takes him all the way.

'We are the perfect partnership,' he says. 'Who knows, we could even make the final. I probably shouldn't say that though because I might jinx it.'

Anton says the Proms queen is quick to pick up the routines. 'We're flying through training, soaring. She cracked the first dance in a matter of days.'

The Kent-born star started dancing at 14, studying contemporary, jazz, ballet and modern theatre dance, as well as being a junior boxer and county footballer. Three years later he decided to specialise in ballroom and, in 1998, he and partner Erin Boag triumphed at the New Zealand Dance Championships, repeating the feat the following year.

Since making the semi-finals in the first-ever *Strictly*, with Lesley Garrett, Anton's longest run has been with series-7 star Laila Rouass, with whom he came fourth. Last year, Anton was paired with Judy Murray but the couple were voted off in Blackpool in week 8.

'Judy was brilliant to work with, a lot of fun, which is what it's all about,' he says. 'We had a lovely time. Well, I did so I hope she did too!

'She's a great girl. We just hung out, had lunch and played a bit of tennis. My forehand came on tremendously. The most famous tennis coach in the UK, giving me lessons on the tennis court – what's not to love?'

Darcey Bussell

As Britain's most famous ballerina, Darcey has played princesses, dying swans and the Sugar Plum Fairy. Having swapped her dancing shoes for the judge's paddle, she hasn't lost her passion for dressing up.

'Coming from the stage I'm quite theatrical when it comes to creating a new style and I get a little bit carried away,' she laughs. 'It's a lovely opportunity because in everyday life – being a mum, taking the kids to school and walking the dog – you don't get that.

'Wearing great clothes makes me feel like a million dollars and it sets the whole scene for what *Strictly* is all about, a little razzmatazz and quality.'

Darcey's theatrical style comes to the fore on themed weekends – although she does occasionally need reining in.

'I love theme weekends because I always get inspired, but I can go too far and I usually have to tone it down,' she admits. 'I like movie night but Halloween is the most fun. I badly want to wear some scary contact lenses and a crazy wig, but I'm not allowed to get too carried away. That's my theatre world coming into it again. I don't have many inhibitions.'

What do you make of the line-up this year?
The atmosphere they have already created with each other is lovely. It has been a lovely surprise and they all seem incredibly excited. It should be a good year.

Who do you have your eye on for the final?
It's far too early to say; they are going to go through so many changes. They each have a long journey.

What is your off-screen style?
I usually go round in either a pair of gym leggings or jeans. I try and smarten it up, occasionally, but usually I'm running in and out of the door doing errands or picking up kids.

What are your favourite things about *Strictly*?
As a dancer, I love the quality of dance and the diversity of it. I love the big group dances. I love the team spirit and how everybody is there for the same goals and to support each other. That is really special and rare. I feel privileged to be on a show that has that camaraderie.

Was Caroline Flack the right winner in series 12?
Definitely. She was a slow builder through the series but she had a quality of leg work, and she was just so professional in the performance. Caroline's showdance was beautiful, and Pasha took a risk. If you do something romantic, fluid and calm, you have to get it right and because they did that, it was unforgettable.

Who made you laugh the most?
Scott Mills. I hated the crab one but I loved his Uncle Fester on Halloween. That was just a joy. Suddenly he got something that he knew what to do with, and he became that person.

You have two daughters. Do they love the show?
They are big fans. My youngest, Zoe, loves the outfits and the themed weekends. She's the dancer of the two so she enjoys trying to copy the steps, while my oldest, Phoebe, likes to see how it's staged, and the music events. They love Bruno's theatricality and they think Craig's antics are really funny.

Ainsley Harriott

Ainsley is used to cooking up a storm in the kitchen but can he put some sauce into a salsa and sizzle in a samba?

'I certainly love a boogie and once the music starts I'm usually one of the first out there on the dance floor,' he says. 'Although I haven't had any formal dance training and something tells me I'm really going to notice the difference!'

The *Ready Steady Cook* host, who is dancing with Natalie Lowe, could have the recipe to make it all the way. He hides a secret pop-star past, having performed in a duo called The Calypso Twins, he's good at thinking on his feet in the kitchen, and he has been known to add a sashay into the mix as he whips up a little something. So he's confident he can handle the strain of the Saturday-night show.

'I don't think anything is more stressful than a kitchen, which is a very unusual place,' he insists. 'It's every day, often twice a day of intense service, that pulsating push to get it right. This is very different and a completely new discipline, but how wonderful to learn a new skill now, in my 50s.'

The flamboyant chef admits he was asked once before to compete on the show, but filming commitments made it impossible.

'If you're going to get involved in this you've got to wipe the diary. You need to train for a minimum of 12 hours a week but if you want to do well, you have to put in six or seven hours a day.'

Now he's on board he can't wait to get into those shimmering Latin costumes.

'I like a bit of sparkle. When do you get a chance to do that if it's not on *Strictly*? I'm pretty exuberant in the kitchen anyway but this is an opportunity to really camp it up, which is great.'

The 58-year-old dad of two is a huge fan of the show and says he has already bonded with his fellow competitors.

'It's such a well-oiled machine and the set is fabulous, the dancers are amazing and within a day or so we were looking after one another, and the camaraderie kicks in quite early. It's almost like you're coming into a party that's been put on several times before.'

So let's get the party started. Ready, Steady, Dance.

Natalie Lowe

Dancing with TV chef Ainsley Harriott, Natalie reckons she has found the recipe for success in her new partner.

'Ainsley has amazing skills,' she enthuses. 'He's got a beautiful natural rhythm, he's a ball of energy, and he's extremely enthusiastic and hard-working. He likes to absorb all my information and take it on board. Every time I correct him he gets better, and he really listens.

'He wants to do well and is learning fast. I love his energy. He comes in the room and he's just beaming from ear to ear. He is the perfect celebrity partner.'

Natalie is hoping Ainsley can add some spice to those sizzling Latin dances, but she reckons she might have to rein him in when it comes to the ballroom numbers.

'He will definitely get his snake hips out,' she laughs. 'He's just got to walk down the corridor and he's wiggling his hips. I have to teach him to keep everything a bit more contained when it comes to the ballroom side of it. But time will tell.'

Natalie's first task was to keep that famous smile off her pupil's face, after being handed a tango as their first dance.

'It's quite a serious dance so he had to keep a straight face,' she says. 'Something fun would have been less challenging but it's all about finding the right balance and producing a fantastic routine. I think he'll be brilliant at finding the right character for each dance. If we give him something to focus on, like a specific character, then I think he'll be able to find his serious side.'

The Australian-born dancer started dancing at the age of 3 and was representing her country at 8. After making a splash in her first series of *Strictly*, dancing with Ricky Whittle, she narrowly lost out on the glitterball to Chris Hollins and Ola Jordan. Last year she only made three rounds with Tim Wonnacott.

'Tim was brilliant,' she recalls. 'He tried his absolute hardest. He'd never danced a day in his life and he really did well but he was up against stiff competition. It was a really strong year but we both had a ball.'

STRICTLY STYLE

For the female celebs, the glitter and glamour is an integral part of the *Strictly* experience. But it's not just the ladies who need to look good on the dance floor. And costume designer Vicky Gill reveals most of the lads soon learn to love being 'Strictlified'.

'At first, the ladies tend to be insecure about aspects of their figures but with the guys it's more about how masculine they'll look,' she says. 'Then suddenly they'll say, "I'm doing this. Get me a frilly shirt!" They very quickly want as many crystals as you can throw at them.'

Those less comfortable with the sparkle and silks of the Latin dances may feel more at home in the traditional tailcoat, which is still the staple of the ballroom wardrobe and cut differently from a standard suit.

'In a normal suit, if you lift your arms the whole jacket moves, but we need a smooth line across the shoulders and arms while in ballroom hold,' explains Vicky. 'The main difference is in the sleeve, because the arm hole is very high under the arm.'

To make sure the jacket doesn't ride up, two lengths of elastic are attached inside, which then button on to the dance trousers, and there's more trickery when it comes to the shirts.

'When the guys go into hold, they can't have a shirt wrinkling at the front,' says Vicky. 'So all the shirts have pants on them that the men step into, like a onesie!'

While the ladies' clothes are made from scratch, the male outfits often come from the fashion stores.

'We buy a lot of high street for the boys because it's closer to what they know. The tailcoats have to be specially made but we can buy slim-fitting trousers, as long as they have a stretch content, and shirts can be customised.'

On the night, every last detail has to be considered, right down to the underwear.

'Studio lighting can go through the fabric and pull colour from underneath, so under a white garment, for instance, we would use a lot of flesh-coloured bases. We may put cycling shorts on so that we don't see any lines.'

The girls traditionally spend more time in wardrobe – but it seems the male celebs are catching up.

'Last year's boys gave the girls a run for their money,' laughs Vicky. 'They were always in wardrobe debating how many sparkles they wanted, or whether they needed to wear a top. Mark Wright made us giggle because he'd try on about eight shirts on a Saturday and always go back to the first one.'

At the risk of upsetting the female audience, Vicky admits that she likes to keep the 'gun shows' to a minimum.

'I know a lot of the ladies watching like to see a bit of muscle on a Saturday night,' she says. 'However, we don't want shirts off every 5 minutes, and sometimes it doesn't make sense. If it works within the number, fine. But if it's just for the sake of getting the six-pack out, it feels wrong.'

Carol Kirkwood

Weather girl Carol is set to bring a ray of sunshine to the *Strictly* dance floor, with her ready smile and warm personality. But she's hoping her dance routines won't be a washout.

'When we're doing the dance in rehearsal it's just us, and even though the cameras are there, you feel like there's no one else watching,' she explains. 'But when it goes live, my fear is that I'll start and then go completely blank.

'You don't want to let anyone down and you don't want to make a fool of yourself and you want to be good. If you can't remember a bit of the routine you feel disappointed in yourself. I'm looking forward to doing it but it's scary that you have to go out there and dance, and every move, every curl of your finger is going to be scrutinised.'

The BBC presenter should be dancing up a storm in the training room, with *Strictly* champ Pasha Kovalev to lead the way. She admits her previous dance experience is minimal. 'I have no dance skills whatsoever,' she says. 'I've done some Scottish country dancing before, which sounds way more glamorous than it is, but it's only really been at weddings; so as for formal dance training, I have none.'

Carol follows in the footsteps of *BBC Breakfast* colleagues Bill Turnbull and 2009 champ Chris Hollins, and says she'll be tapping them up for advice in her bid for final glory. But she's not forecasting a triumph just yet.

'I'm quite competitive in the sense that I want to do well, but I'm also a realist,' she reasons. 'I'm 53 and probably not the fittest person you are ever going to meet, so I don't fancy my chances but I'm going to give it everything I have.'

'I would like to make it to the final and be holding that glitterball trophy but whether I will or not is another matter.'

The hard-working star will carry on delivering the daily weather reports throughout the series and jokes, 'Goodness knows how I'll cope. I'm going to look like Deputy Dawg.'

But she's praying her TV colleagues will drop the gags once she starts competing.

She laughs: 'Everyone keeps saying to me, "Do you want a cup of cha-cha-cha?"'

Pasha Kovalev

Reigning champ Pasha returns with a sunny disposition and a weather girl on his arm. But will Carol Kirkwood be a whirlwind on the dance floor? It won't be for the want of trying.

'Carol has thrown herself into it and her enthusiasm is brimming over,' Pasha says. 'She doesn't want to stop dancing. She is really excited and she's putting all her energy into it.'

But the Siberian star admits that Carol's lack of experience on the dance floor means there's plenty of work to be done.

'We started off a bit wobbly, as it always is at the beginning stage of dancing,' he says. 'We have to do everything from scratch. I told her we have to build a basement before we can start building a house on top of it.'

But Pasha promises to keep the sunny smile on Carol's face for as many dances as possible.

Last year's final saw Pasha and partner Caroline Flack clinch the glitterball trophy with a stunning showdance and a sizzling salsa, which they repeated on this year's launch show.

'It felt like we'd never had a break,' he reveals. 'We fell straight back into the partnership and it felt good. Obviously there's a bit of pressure because someone is coming back as the champion, but it was really great because we pulled it all together and it showed everyone that she hasn't lost it yet.'

Talking of losing it, Pasha admits to a nasty moment after last year's grand final when he thought he'd actually lost his precious prize.

'Caroline stole my glitterball!' he laughs. 'We were given little replica trophies, because the main one doesn't leave the studio, and at the wrap party, when I was about to go home, my bag was missing. My glitterball had been sticking out, clearly visible, so nobody could have thought it was their bag. But it was gone, with the glitterball, and I was starting to get upset.

'Then I got a text from Caroline saying, "My sister saw the glitterball and thought it was my bag so she took it." Luckily, I got it back and it's now on the shelf, glinting in the sunshine.'

Carol would no doubt approve.

STRICTLY SPOOKY

Fright Night at *Strictly* is always a scream. The competing couples become glamorous ghouls and sparkling spooks for their hair-raising Halloween routines, and the live audience braves the bawl-room for a feast of spine-chilling sambas, frightening foxtrots and petrifying paso dobles. Welcome to the house of horror, as we mingle with the vampires and zombies in our backstage special.

9.20 a.m. There's no rest for the wicked on Halloween and hair supervisor Neale Pirie has been on the go since the crack of dawn. 'I was the first one in, at 7.30,' he reveals. 'We have so many concepts on a theme night, so there's a lot to do. This morning was spent colouring wigs and getting everything ready.

'The first dancers and celebs begin to arrive about nine o'clock, and from then on it doesn't stop. It's a big blur of people coming in and out, and just keeps going and going. It's full on, but I'd never want to be anywhere else on a Saturday!'

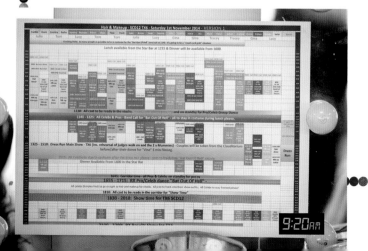

10 a.m. The make-up and hair room has filled with excited chatter as the celeb dancers and their professional partners begin their macabre makeovers. Ola Jordan is being smothered in black-and-white make-up, for a skeletal look, and her hair is being fashioned into a bone. Frankie Bridge has taken a new twist on the traditional fake tan by going green for her *Wicked* tango. 'She's got to stay green all day,' laughs partner Kevin Clifton. 'She looks great.' The make-up team are hand-brushing the body paint on to the singer's skin, after airbrushing attempts failed.

'My hands have to be green as well as my face and my back too,' explains Frankie 'because my dress has a massive hole in the back.'

The Saturdays star admits to frustration during training, but she reckons Kevin is keeping her on track. 'He never gets angry or frustrated, or if he does he hides it well. We laugh a lot and he's very laid-back, which stops me from getting stressed out.'

10.30 a.m. Throughout the morning each couple is given a 10 minute slot to run through their routine in the studio. Joanne Clifton and Scott Mills are going through the paces of their Addams Family foxtrot, complete with a disembodied hand to click them in and out. 'I think they did auditions for the hand' laughs Joanne later. 'Matt Howes, the music producer, got it because he has timing.'

10.50 a.m. Janette Manrara is beginning her transformation for her *Sleepy Hollow*-style paso doble to 'Black Betty'. With two group dances on the cards, each of the pro dancers will have three different looks tonight. 'We don't have time to change the make-up between dances because we are live, so we have to work around hiding things,' says hair and make-up designer Lisa Armstrong. 'For the first number, "Bat Out of Hell", they're wearing hoods, so they can hide their costumes underneath. They will have black lipstick, and when that dance is over, the lipstick comes off, and the make-up is already complete for their couple's dance. After that we have "Sweet Dreams", where Janette is Snow White, so she'll just have a lip change, and we may take the lashes off. Then they all go back to their couple look for the results.'

11.20 a.m. There's great excitement as two Dalmatians, brought in for Anton Du Beke and Judy Murray's Cruella de Vil routine, arrive on set. Professional pooches Macey and Connie pull off their rehearsal with perfect timing.

11:30AM

1.40 p.m. The dancing kicks off with Alison Hammond descending from the rafters on a swing for her 'Wuthering Heights' American smooth. Partner Aljaž Skorjanec – a mean and moody Heathcliff – later admits he knows little about Emily Brontë's classic love story. 'I just learnt how to say Heathcliff!' he laughs. 'I don't know the book too well.'

He was relieved it was Alison, not him, on the swing. 'We had a trial at the beginning of the week, and I tried it,' he says. 'It's quite scary! It moves. It doesn't just hold still. I couldn't do it.'

1.55 p.m. The skirt on Kristina's outfit is trailing on the floor, and wardrobe assistants are on hand to make a quick adjustment before she can rehearse her spider-themed paso.

2.05 p.m. Disaster strikes as Ola's outfit gets caught up with Steve Backshall's during an ambitious lift.

2.30 p.m. Jake Wood and Janette's enthusiastic paso has unravelled her horns, which Neale Pirie had fashioned from Janette's own hair.

11.30 a.m. Back in make-up, Joanne Clifton is becoming Morticia Addams, Caroline Flack is a disco-dancing zombie, and Pixie Lott is having gruesome raw-flesh prosthetics applied for her terrifying tango. 'I love Halloween week,' says Lisa. 'You get to be really creative and do things you can't do any other week.'

12.05 p.m. The whole cast is on set rehearsing their group number. Janette is dancing in comfy boots while Kristina Rihanoff manages the whole routine in high-heeled slippers. Anton's first attempt to fly over the other dancers, dressed as Count Dracula, ends with him spinning in the air above their heads amid a lot of laughter.

1.30 p.m. Tess and stand-in presenter Zoe Ball take to the stage for the all-important dress rehearsal. Everyone is on set except for the judges, who are replaced by crew members.

12:05PM

1:40 pm

'I like this stage of the day,' says director of choreography Jason Gilkison. 'I've done my bit and it's out of my hands, so I can relax, watch the show, and then it all starts again tomorrow.'

But for the celebs, and their pro tutors, it's the most nerve-wracking time of the day – and Joanne Clifton is fretting because partner Scott, usually a bundle of nerves, has been getting it right!

'It's quite scary because this is the first week that Scott hasn't made any mistakes, either yesterday or today,' she laughs. 'Normally he gets it right all week then we get to Elstree and he messes it up, but he's got it all right so far and that's quite scary.'

5.35 p.m. The audience are in the auditorium, and the performers are in their dressing rooms or trying to grab some last-minute practice in the corridors. The backstage buzz heightens as the live show approaches.

6.30 p.m. The familiar strains of the theme music can be heard backstage as the couples wait to go on. Da da, da da, da, da, da … Da da, da da, da. Show time!

3.30 p.m. In wardrobe, Len Goodman has just popped in for an adjustment to his suit and Steve is stripping off for some speedy alterations to his skeleton outfit which the dressers sort out. The dress run has thrown up a couple of issues, including Ola's mishap.

'We took all the buttons off Steve's costume because we were worried about Ola getting caught, but there was a hook on his cummerbund, at the back,' explains wardrobe's Theresa Hewlett. 'As she spun round him part of her skirt got caught on him. She had a knotted fringe so we have undone the knots, and that should solve it.

'Also Alison has floats on her shoulders, which detached when she took her cloak off. Because it's Halloween they are raw edged and quite weak. So we have a bit of last-minute sewing on that too, but that's why dress rehearsals happen.'

5 p.m. Most of the cast are taking a break refuelling from the buffet for the gruelling night ahead.

5:00 pm

GET THE STRICTLY

It might be the scariest night of the year, but ghoulish can still be glamorous. So ditch the witch hat, dump the Dracula cape and make a Halloween hullabaloo with our *Strictly* stunning makeover, as modelled by Janette Manrara.

Janette's series 12 paso doble, with Jake Wood, was based on a theme, with a fiery horse running through sinister woods and fog billowing around the couple. The Halloween themes allow the stylists to let their imaginations run wild.

'My inspiration comes from the concept and the dance style,' explains hair and make-up designer, Lisa Armstrong. 'So Janette chose a theme, and I take it from that, from the dress and from the dance. We went for a -style Victorian look with bright pinks and reds on the eyes, then pale skin, massive lashes and a two-tone lip in black and red.'

While the look can be wildly different to the usual sparkle, Lisa is careful not to go too far. 'We have to be true to our audience, and we know that there are young children watching, so we don't want to be too scary,' she says. 'We want to create characters rather than turning everyone into a wicked witch or a zombie. With Janette we wanted to make her look doll-like, and that's where the fun element came across.'

Make-up by Lisa Armstrong

'We went completely against the grain of the normal make-up. Everything is paler and more ghoulish, and the features are highlighted, so we put more emphasis and structure on the brow bone, the cheekbone and the jawbone to get that hollow look. Janette is very pixie-like anyway, with tiny features, so that's quite easy to create.'

HALLOWEEN LOOK

To break up the colours and give a sunken look, add black eyeshadow along the socket line then thick black eyeliner on the lash line.

Now attach those big lashes. They draw you to the eyes and help with the overall oddity of the look, which is something you need to embrace at Halloween. They are available to buy in many high-street stores, as well as online.

With a black eyeliner, draw a little heart on your cheek and colour in with a red lip liner.

For the two-tone lips, outline the lips with a red lip liner to create the shape, going from the outer corner to the middle, top and bottom. Repeat on the other side. Then draw a black line right into the pout of the lip, with a black eye pencil. Fill in the black with the eye pencil and then, with the red lipstick, fill in the middle section.

TO DO AT HOME

1. Start with a foundation two shades lighter than your usual colour.

2. Use a dark brown or black eyeshadow and blusher brush to contour, sweeping underneath the brow bone, the cheekbone and the jawbone, to create that sunken, ghoulish look.

3. We wouldn't normally wear a bright pink with a bright red on the eye, but this is Halloween! Apply the pink all across the eyelid then a swathe of red to the socket and up to the brow.

Tip: 'I used loose powder called a pigment, because it is true to form, so what you see in the pot is the colour that will transfer on to the skin. Pressed powders look beautiful and bright in their packaging, but when you apply to the skin, the colour becomes weak.'

Hair by Neale Pirie

Hair supervisor Neale Pirie fashioned Janette's mass of long hair into horns, for a devilish look.

'Because it was *Sleepy Hollow* we didn't want it to be all groomed and perfect,' he reveals. 'It needed to be a bit more organic and lived in. So we didn't want a typical horn shape. We wanted a nod to that vibe but still quite wearable and sassy.'

On this occasion, Janette ended up with smaller horns than planned because the first style unravelled in dress rehearsal, but the size can be varied to suit your look.

'Janette is so full-on when she dances, she's like a bullet, so anything that extends too far out of the head for her becomes an issue, and gravity takes its toll,' says Neale. 'But she looked amazing that day.'

TO DO AT HOME

1. Loosely tong the hair and then tousle with the hand so it is a messy wave rather than a perfect curl.

2. For each horn, put the hair into a band, like a pigtail, then backcomb it. Fold the hair over into a horn shape and place another band over the first band to hold it in place.

3. Wrap what's left of the hair round the horn shape that you've made. Fix the style with pins and a LOT of hairspray. Short kirby grips are best because they are easier to hide underneath the structure of the horn.

Tip: 'We used quite a lot of dry shampoo in the hair so it was nice and textured; if you take away the horns, the hair is actually very fashionable.'

Dressing Up by Vicky Gill

Costume queen Vicky came up with a stunning black outfit for Janette's *Sleepy Hollow* scarefest.

'I answered the brief with a black georgette peasant sleeve inserted into a black sequin catsuit base, with a circular frill detail running through the costume. We then used bands of georgette, satin, mesh and chiffon to make a full skirt, which was attached to the catsuit to maintain the volume and movement required for the paso.

'Appropriately for Halloween, the traditional name for this skirt is a broomstick, although we would now call it a peasant or gypsy tiered skirt.'

TO DO AT HOME

1. Dig out an old black blouse and tiered skirt or pick them up at a charity shop.

2. If you can't find anything black, use black dye.

3. Add black lace round the cuffs and hems, and wherever else you see fit, then get ripping.

> **Tip:** 'Halloween is an opportunity to go a little mad. Go wild, don't be afraid to chop, slash and rip. After all, anything goes. Have fun!'

Anthony Ogogo

oxing is all about fancy footwork and Olympic medallist Anthony is hoping to be the first fighter to make it to the final. But he may have to put the lifts on hold for the first few weeks, after kicking off the series with an injury.

'In my last fight, six weeks before *Strictly*, I dislocated my shoulder,' he explains. 'I carried on fighting and I won the fight, which was good, but I had an operation on it and I can't fight until January. So when I was asked if I wanted to do the show, I thought I could either sit at home doing nothing for three months or I could go on the biggest TV programme in the country and have a lot of fun. It was a no-brainer really.

'I'm now out of the sling and getting stronger, and hopefully by week 3 I'll be back to full fitness and can fling my partner around. But I'm taking it seriously and I want to be as good as I possibly can.'

Anthony bagged a bronze for Britain in the 2012 Olympics and since turning professional in the same year he has never lost a fight. But can he go three rounds with Craig?

'As a boxer, I'm always doing things wrong,' he reasons. 'My coach is always

telling me off or shouting at me. I've got used to it. So if I'm getting slated by Craig, I'll probably agree.'

Whatever the judges' verdict, the 26-year-old will be keeping his fists to himself.

'I'd be the last person to fight back. If you're a chef and cook all day you don't want to come home and cook for the family. So I'm the most laidback, passive person on the planet. I get enough violence in my chosen sport!'

Teamed with new girl Oti Mabuse, Anthony couldn't have been happier. 'There aren't enough superlatives in the world to describe Oti,' he says. 'I'm over the moon.'

He's hoping his dancing will be knockout, and his family are in his corner – even if they find the whole thing hilarious.

'I have a mum and four sisters, so I grew up in a houseful of women, and they all watch the show,' he reveals. 'But they laughed when I told them, because I'm not synonymous with dancing. My older sister told me she loves *Strictly* and sometimes she gets so emotional over the dances, she cries.'

'She won't be crying when I start dancing. She'll be laughing her head off.'

Oti Mabuse

Newcomer Oti will have to box clever to get partner Anthony Ogogo through the first few rounds. His dislocated shoulder meant their debut dance, a jive, was a real challenge.

'Anthony couldn't really move his arm in rehearsal so it had to stay in the same place,' she reveals. 'But he's willing to do everything else that I ask of him. He's a good student. He picked up the first steps really well.'

The stunning South African was born in Pretoria and took up ballroom dancing as a child along with her sister, now a judge on the German version of *Strictly*. After winning eight Latin American Championships in her own country, she moved to Germany and later competed on the German show with pop star Daniel Küblböck.

She's excited to be joining the UK show and says the other dancers have welcomed her with open arms.

'Everybody is so nice, easy-going and respectful that it's wonderfully easy to fit in,' she says. 'They look after me like I'm their baby sister. It's been great. The girls have been great at giving me advice and the boys have really been lovely to me.'

Oti is hoping her quickstepping partner can break the line of *Strictly* boxers with two left feet.

'From what I've seen so far, he really can move. He wants to do well, he wants to work hard and he wants to learn.'

She says the pair got on so well the first time they met, before the launch show, that she thought they may be laughing too much in rehearsals to get much work done. But sicne traning began, she says, it's all falling into place.

'I can be a strict teacher but with Anthony there's no need because he's such a great student, and so willing to learn, that I am patient and kind all the time.'

But she's making sure she keeps a steady stream of snacks on hand.

'The only time I heard a complaint in the first rehearsal was when he was hungry,' she laughs. 'I felt his energy sap so I said, "What happened? Your energy just dropped to minus seven." So he said, "I'm hungry." We had some lunch and he was fine, a changed man. So I just have to keep feeding him and then I can get him to do what I want.'

Bruno Tonioli

The flamboyant Italian is rarely lost for words but he's stumped when it comes to predicting the finalists from our latest bunch of new recruits.

'It's very different this series,' he says. 'It's one of the most interesting and potentially even seasons we've ever had. It's a very wide open field.'

'The good thing about *Strictly* is that you never know what is going to happen. That's part of the appeal. Every season is different and the judges are like the public: we're ready to discover new delights every time.'

Even so, Bruno confesses to being as nervous as the celebrities in the run-up to the new series.

'It's always nerve-racking doing the live show because you don't know what is going to happen,' he explains. 'But it's going to be very exciting because it's so unpredictable.'

Did you spot any potential champs in the group dance?

It's impossible to spot anything in the group dance. It's such a mess. They've only just met and they're very nervous, they've never done it before; so it's hard for us to make up our minds from that. You have to give them a chance. They need a couple of weeks.

What do you make of the line-up?

The girls all look fit, bright and smart. We've got some very fit guys too. We have Ainsley Harriott, the funny man, but I think he's going to be quite good. I don't think he's going to be just a joke.

I think some of the girls could do very well, but which ones, without seeing the dances, I can't tell. They've all got the right equipment but it's very open. There's no one there who doesn't have the potential, so the leader board could change every week.

Anyone there who you think will struggle?

There no one about whom I would say, It's just not going to work, but we don't have a Pixie Lott either, where you know she's going to do well. There's no Judy Murray. Then again I haven't seen them do a couples dance yet. They might be dreadful!

Is Anton in with a chance this year?

He's got to get it together now because Katie Derham looks good, and she's smart, and beautiful. His ballroom has always been great but now he has an opportunity to show that off instead of being the comedy act. Mind you, we like his jokes. I'll never forget his routines with Judy and I couldn't wait to see what they did next. Judy embraced the craziness of it all and that's what made it so appealing.

What did you make of the final last year?

Caroline was great. She was wonderful, hard-working, determined; she deserved to win. I would have liked to have seen Pixie in the final, but sadly the dance-off meant she was out. Shame.

Helen George

Actress Helen is best known for bringing babies into the world in *Call the Midwife*, but can she deliver a decent foxtrot or a jumping jive?

'I did ballet when I was younger but I think that could be a bit of a hindrance as it is so different from all of the ballroom and Latin dances that I will have to do on *Strictly*,' she says. 'We did learn a bit of swing dancing on *Call the Midwife*, which was really fun, and there was a lot of partner work so I got to do upside-down lifts. I'm excited about being thrown around the room and things like that.'

The 31-year-old actress recently trained for the London Marathon, so fitness isn't a problem. She's even lapping up the tough training regime.

'There was so much concentration in the room when we did the group training, because we all want to do the best that we can do, and I think we're all a bit intimidated. But I've been smiling so much since we started. I'm just loving it. I love the physical exertion of it.'

But she admits she's in awe of the professionals after watching them at work. 'The dancers are so gorgeous I can't take my eyes off them – and that's the women. The six-packs on these girls! When they're all together in costume they look like some amazing superhero team. They're gods.'

Helen's family and friends are thrilled she's doing the show, and co-star Miranda Hart – a huge *Strictly* fan – is dancing with delight.

'I've had an amazing reaction,' laughs Helen. 'You can do anything with your career but as soon as you mention this everybody says, "Wow, you're doing *Strictly*!" Before the launch Miranda was texting me for all the gossip, asking, "Who's your partner going to be?" She is really excited.'

While her acting experience may give her the edge when it comes to performance, Helen, who is dancing with Aljaž Škorjanec, admits being out of character is what worries her most.

'I think that's what I find quite nerve-racking,' she says. 'Suddenly you're having to be yourself and the actors in the group are really struggling with that. Even just talking down the camera instead of talking to someone else is strange so I'm nervous about that.'

Aljaž Škorjanec

On his *Strictly* debut two years ago, Aljaž and partner Abbey Clancy romped home to take the trophy. But can he nurse *Call the Midwife* star Helen George to the final and become the first-ever double winner?

'A couple of people have asked me that already but to be honest I haven't even put one thought into it,' says the modest pro. 'Every year I take it week by week and try to teach my partner the best and most beautiful routines I can come up with, and if they can have fun while they're doing it, I'm winning every single week.'

The slinky Slovenian is pleased with his new pupil and thinks she has the potential to go far.

'It's early days but I think she could be really good,' he reveals. 'She moves well. I am glad we started with a waltz because she looks good in hold and I'm more of a ballroom boy, so happy days.'

'I was happy when we got partnered up,' he says. 'She is great to be around, she's really funny and we're going to get along really well.'

As Helen is filming the next series of *Call the Midwife,* training will have to be slotted around her busy schedule, but Aljaž is relaxed.

'We should be fine,' he insists. 'I'm going to make the most of the time that we get so we'll be as ready as we can.'

Last year, Aljaž partnered *Strictly* showstopper Alison Hammond to week 7, and the pair got on like a house on fire.

'That was probably the best experience ever in my life,' he says. 'Spending so much time with someone so positive and so nice was wonderful. I had an absolute ball and I was sad when we got eliminated, but now it's a new year and a new challenge.'

Another new challenge awaits after the series ends, as he's planning his wedding to fellow pro Janette Manrara. The couple announced their engagement this summer.

'It sort of happened when we were just kicking off rehearsals with *Strictly* so we have no time to plan anything other than a dance every week,' Aljaž explains. 'For now, we're going to focus on the show, which pretty much takes every hour of our day!'

Lord of the
DANCE

As Director of Choreography, **JASON GILKISON** is the man behind many a move on the *Strictly* dance floor. As well as offering advice and support to the pro dancers for their couple's routines, the award-winning Australian oversees the professional and celebrity group dances and choreographs half of them himself.

'There are around 21 or 22 group numbers per series and often another pro dance to accompany the guest artist, so we delegate,' he explains. 'I'll take ten of the routines and then we hand out the rest to great choreographers, who usually do one or two each. That way, as the series gets more intense, I have more time to devote to helping the couples with their dances.'

For Jason, the *Strictly* year begins in June, when he gets together with the production team to plot the group dances for the whole series. After his fellow choreographers are booked and briefed, the team get down to the serious business of plotting the dances and themes for the entire series.

'We don't know who the celebrities are at

this point,' says Jason. 'So we start to come up with random concepts, which also go in the pot. Then we start to compile big lists of what might work. Sometimes we have a hint of the occupation of some of our celebrities. For instance, when we had Deborah Meaden we listed songs that worked with female businesswomen, including 'It's a Man's Man's World', 'She Works Hard for the Money' and so on. Once we know who the celebrities are, it becomes much easier.'

The former Latin champ starts putting the pros through their paces in early August, getting a head start on the group dances before they pair up with their celebrity partners. As well as having dancing feet, the 15 pros dancers need to be on their toes in terms of memory.

'There's a different routine every day, and they learn about 80 per cent of the dances they will do for the rest of the series,' reveals Jason. 'But by the time we revisit them, it can be two months on, and they only have a couple of rehearsals to relearn each one. Monday can be quite a tough day.'

Jason's own dance-floor pedigree means he has plenty of experience to draw on for the show. With long-term dance partner Peta Roby, he created one of Australia's most successful dance partnerships, becoming undefeated Latin champions from 1981 to 1997 and taking the British, world and international titles. He moved on to direct the hit stage show *Burn the Floor*, and after a stint as choreographer and judge on *So You Think You Can Dance*, in both Australia and the USA, he joined the *Strictly* family.

Although the celebrity routines are down to the professionals, the dances are mapped out at the beginning of the series after discussions with everyone involved.

'We talk to them all one by one, saying, for example, "We think you should go for this track for the salsa"; "How do you feel about the paso doble for Blackpool?" and so on.

'We come up with the music and lots of concepts, so then we'll say, "We'd love someone this series to do …" For instance, last year, the Halloween routine to "Defying Gravity" was discussed by a few dancers before it eventually landed with Frankie and Kevin."'

Once the triumphs and travails of the live show are over, Jason is planning the following week's routine.

'I love that each week Monday is a fresh start and you can say, "That didn't work too well. Let's not do that again," or "That worked really well." You work hard and you get to the Saturday, and then you have to start all over again.'

But the choreographer king is never nervous about potential dance-floor disasters.

'For me, that's the attraction of the show,' he laughs. 'It's not clean and tidy and perfect. It can go wrong. That's natural, and these things happen, but the fact that someone's routine didn't go too well often causes them to come back stronger the following week.'

Globe Trotters

Ballroom dance is a truly international affair, with more than 30 countries regularly competing at the highest level. Naturally, the *Strictly* pro line-up reflects the sport, with top talent gleaned from all over the globe coming together to form their own world of dance.

UK – Anton Du Beke, Kevin Clifton, Joanne Clifton

It may not be taught in every school, but Blighty can hold her own in the world of dance. Popularity of classes and social dances has shot up in recent years, and British couples have been World Ballroom Champions for 77 of the 91 years since the competition began. Bournemouth and Blackpool are renowned for international contests, including the World Championships and the annual Blackpool Dance Festival.

USA – Janette Manrara

The US has a long love affair with ballroom, dating back to the 1900s, when dancers Irene and Vernon Castle were huge celebrities and popularised the waltz, tango and quickstep. Californian Harry Fox introduced the foxtrot in 1914 and the Charleston followed in the 1920s. The following decade saw the rise of Fred Astaire, and the American smooth-style dance routines, and the jive and Lindy Hop were all the rage in the '50s. Today the competitive circuit benefits from both home-grown talent and dancers trained in other parts of the world, including current World Champions Arūnas Bižokas and Katusha Demidova.

South America Venezuela – Karen Hauer

Partner dancing is a long tradition in this South American country where the national dance since 1882 has been the waltz-like Joropo – meaning 'party'. The Venezuelan merengue and the polka are also popular.

South Africa – Otlile Mabuse

A nation steeped in rhythm and movement, South Africa was introduced to the more formal dances of ballroom by the colonial powers in the 1900s, and the competitive scenes thrived through the 1920s. Apartheid saw a dip in the sport, through social division, but in the 1990s ballroom became the fastest-growing pastime among children of the deprived townships and it remains hugely popular today.

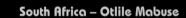

Ireland – Tristan MacManus

It's not all Riverdance in the Emerald Isle. Since the 1980s, Dance Sport has become increasingly popular, spreading from its original hotspot of Dublin to wider regions. Tristan's appearance last year brought ballroom fever in Ireland to a whole new level.

Western Europe
Italy – Giovanni Pernice

Italy is home to some of the most highly respected dance schools in the world and our own Joanne Clifton moved to Bologna at 14 to train, as did Sicilian-born Giovanni. Ballroom and Latin are often taught in schools and FIDS, the Italian Dance Sport Federation, has more than 100,000 members.

Slovenia – Aljaž Skorjanec

Dance Sport is a popular pastime in the former Yugoslavian state for both boys and girls. Aljaž started competing at five and has 19 Slovenian championships to his name. In 2014, Slovenia became the 50th country to license the *Strictly Come Dancing* format.

Eastern Europe
Poland – Ola Jordan

As in many parts of Eastern Europe, ballroom dancing in Poland is as common as other sports and is often taught in schools. Former champ Ola started at ten and a teacher at her school spotted her talent. The World Latin Dance Champions in 2008 and 2009 were Polish.

Russia – Aliona Vilani and Gleb Savchenko
Siberia – Pasha Kovalev and Kristina Rihanoff

With dancing part of the national curriculum from pre-school up, it's no surprise the ballroom scene thrives in Russia. Dance is treated as a serious sport rather than a pastime and all our Russian stars began competing at a young age. The current World Latin number one, Yulia Zagoruychenko, hails from the country.

Australia – Natalie Lowe

Competitive ballroom, now known as Dance Sport, is hugely popular in Australia, where the age categories for competitors stretch from the under 13s to the over 50s. As well as the standard and Latin dances, the sport includes 15 'New Vogue' sequence dances, where all the couples on the floor dance the same steps. Australia also brought us the seminal dance movie, *Strictly Ballroom*.

New Zealand – Brendan Cole

As well as giving us our series 1 champ and past pros Hayley Holt and Erin Boag, the New Zealand dance circuit led to careers for Brendan's older brother Scott and younger sister Vanessa.

Daniel O'Donnell

With a career spanning 30 years and hundreds of sell-out concerts under his belt, Daniel is no stranger to performing and has even been known to dance on stage. But he insists *Strictly* is a whole new chapter.

'With the bit of dancing I've done on stage, I don't have to be in a particular place at a particular time, so I never do the same thing two nights running,' he explains. 'But with this sort of dancing, if you're not hitting your mark, you've messed up. That's a big challenge. It's not just jigging away like I've done before.'

The Irish crooner, who has been paired with Kristina Rihanoff, is a hard worker with an amazing 47 albums to his name. Having known the sweet taste of success, he's giving it his all in a bid to grab that glitterball.

'Everybody wants to be in the final,' he says. 'We're not here to lose. Anybody that succeeds in life is never a loser. But at the end of the day, this is not what we do, so if we get any distance at all, that's great.

'I just hope I stay long enough to learn how to dance. If I can get up on the floor and do a perfect waltz or a cha-cha-cha, I'll be happy.'

The 53-year-old from Donegal promises he will take the judges' verdict on the chin.

'You just have to realise that they know what they're talking about,' he says. 'We're doing something that we've never done before, and they're going to try and make it better.'

The first step on Daniel's steep *Strictly* learning curve was a trip to the tanning booth, which came as something of a shock.

'I didn't even realise the men had spray tans,' laughs Daniel. 'I never even thought about it and then we got a little note saying that Friday was spray-tan day.'

'There's a first time for everything and if that's what it takes, that's what it takes.'

Kristina Rihanoff

The Siberian dancer has landed herself the luck of the Irish for this year's competition, partnering silky-voiced crooner Daniel O'Donnell. And she's thrilled with the partnership.

'I'm so happy to have been paired with Daniel,' she says. 'I was hoping it would be him because he impressed me in the group rehearsals. He really picked up the ballroom quickly and was great in hold. He has great poise, and as a singer he can hear the music, which really helps with timing.'

Although Kristina is not planning to dance to any of Daniel's many popular tracks, she has plenty of creative routines for the Irish idol, and she is sure to please the legion of female fans backing him to win.

'Daniel is a truly lovely person and very respectful to the ladies,' she reveals. 'I have met his wife, Majella, and his brother and the family are all friendly and very supportive. We are going to have a lot of fun.'

Kristina began dancing as a child, in Siberia, and was teaching Latin and ballroom by the age of 15. After moving to the US at 21, she worked on the *Dancing with the Stars* tour, as well as choreographing *So You Think You Can Dance* and starring in the West End in *Burn the Floor*.

She has been part of the *Strictly* family since 2008, when she won the nation's heart with stomping John Sergeant. Last year saw her get the closest yet to the glitterball trophy, finishing as runner-up with Blue star Simon Webbe. It wasn't an easy ride, as the couple survived the dance-off three times along the way.

'To go from lots of dance-offs into the final was amazing. After being in the bottom two I didn't think we'd make it to the final, and that made him improve. I'm really happy that he came out of it so well.'

MUSIC MAESTRO

from the opening bars of the familiar theme tune to the final showdance, live music is an integral part of the *Strictly* experience. With 15 dance styles and more than 160 tracks played throughout the series, the talented singers and orchestra have to be prepared for anything.

But the incredible 90-second arrangements that fill the dance floor on Saturday nights are not put together in a week. Every single note that is played marks months of preparation, wrangling and organisation.

'I have so many spreadsheets you wouldn't believe it,' laughs music producer **MATTHEW HOWES**. 'I have a record of every track ever used on the show, and lists of potential tracks, plus special tracks for Halloween, Christmas etc.'

'We have a loose rule that we can't reuse anything from the last two or three years, or ever if a routine is particularly memorable, such as Ann Widdecombe's "My Heart Will Go On". We would never do that again because it's legendary. If we

did, it would have to be a very different version.'

The process of choosing the tracks begins in June, when the pro dancers each submit a list of preferences. But clashes with other dancers mean they are not able to get all their choices, and the unveiling of their celebrity partner can change everything.

'There are sometimes huge hits that half of the pros might want to dance to. "Happy" by Pharrell Williams is a good example because there aren't many modern jives, so we knew we would be using that, and in the end Tristan got it. There's a bit of juggling because you don't want any of the dancers to get none of the songs they really want, while another gets lots.'

Matthew has a hands on approach to the job – he proved perfect to play Thing in Jo and Scott's Addams Family routine.

The Titanic theme could sail again, but only on a very different course.

The team also has to make sure the music and dance styles are varied enough to keep the viewers on their toes.

'The dancers may have brilliant ideas for a track but it might not work for that particular show,' says Matthew. 'For example, two people might want to do a big-band number. I talk to production and we come up with alternative ideas, and then I talk to the professional dancers and try to work out something that everybody is happy with, so every song brings something different to the show.

'If you ended up with three pasos, for instance, that would feel too samey, so we try to spread the dances, the tempos, the energy and the decade from which the music is chosen.'

With six days a week in training, it's also essential that the couples don't get sick of the music.

'Sometimes a celebrity might have a negative reaction to a song, and we don't want somebody stuck with a song they're not going to enjoy for an entire week!'

Once the music is finalised, Matthew creates a 90-second edit for the professional. 'It might go backwards and forwards a couple of times while they get the bits that they really want,' he explains.

Tristan was 'Happy' to land Pharrell's catchy hit for his jive with Jenny Gibney.

'There can be a specific part where they have a certain move in mind, so we work together to get the edit they want. Then I take it to Dave Arch, the arranger and musical director, and say, "Can you play it?" The answer is always yes because Dave can do anything. He is a stone-cold genius!'

DANCING SHOES

As all dancers know, fancy footwork requires fancy footwear. The stunning shoes pounding the floor every Saturday night are more than a fashion statement. In fact, they are a vital piece of sports equipment, as Justin Patel, from specialists International Dance Shoes (IDS), is all too aware.

'Dance shoes have to be as light and as flexible as possible,' he explains. 'They have to be perfectly balanced, incredibly comfortable, very secure and strong. And they have to look great.'

Because of the unique properties required in the shoe, the materials used differ from high-street styles.

'The sole is suede leather, which enables the dancer to move the way they want to,' reveals Justin. 'Ballroom dancers need a gliding motion and Latin dancers need the shoe to stick a bit more, so they rough up the sole to get more friction. We

use a lot of sport-based materials because dancers are athletes. So there are microfibres inside, to absorb sweat, and the cushioning is similar to that used in high-end trainers, but even more lightweight and streamlined because they need to look elegant.

'The shoes need to hug the feet and can't be at all bulky, either in the look or the feel.'

Over the course of each series, IDS, founded by Justin's father, Rashmi, in 1981, supplies the show with around 450 pairs of shoes. Most of them will be standard lines from the Milton Keynes factory, which can be customised with crystals and sequins by the wardrobe department. However, there will be the occasional request that requires a more bespoke approach.

'Sometimes someone is wearing a fluorescent blue or pink dress and they want matching shoes, so we use the exact material they use on the dress,' says Justin. 'Some people have a wide front of the foot but a narrower back, or vice versa, and we can cater for that.'

And recent experience proves that no job is too big for the master shoemakers.

'Audley Harrison had size 16 feet, which is the biggest shoe we've ever made. I could literally fit my arms into them. They all had to be hand cut, hand mastered and stitched by hand. We even had to make our own shoe box so that we could put them in something to get them to him.'

As the celebrities need proper dance shoes before they start training, Justin and his team are on hand during the early wardrobe fittings to take measurements and offer a selection of styles. But when the long hours of rehearsals kick in, the initial fit often has to be reviewed.

'The celebrities learn more about their feet as they go on,' says Justin. 'In the last series, Sunetra Sarker's feet began to swell up and she had a few blisters, so we tried a couple of different pairs to gauge the size she needed to change to. They start off with what we recommend from the measurements, but then if they feel their feet need more space, or they prefer things a bit tighter, then we change things.'

A special shoe order can usually be turned around in less than a day, which is crucial to the tight *Strictly* schedule. And it's not just the dancers who like the bespoke nature of the footwear from IDS.

'Bruce Forsyth loves our shoes, and he now has a pair of lasts [foot moulds] at our factory, so when he wants a new pair he calls Rashmi, and we make them to the exact mould of his feet.'

Mark Wright had bespoke white brogues made up for the final showdance.

'When Simon Webbe did his Charleston with Kristina he wore black-and-white brogues and we made a matching white patent sandal with a black T-bar for Kristina.'

Dancing shoes stacked up and ready to be shipped to the *Strictly* studio.

'Thom Evans danced the foxtrot in a tweed waistcoat, so we made up a matching pair of brogues in beige and navy. Pasha wore the other ones for his quickstep with Caroline.'

Jamelia

Singer Jamelia went from chart success to becoming a darling of daytime TV on *Loose Women*. But it's the glitz and glamour of the whole *Strictly* experience that has got her pulse racing.

'The more things we do – whether it's trying on shoes, putting on a dress or going into a sparkly ballroom – the more the excitement is building,' she says. 'At the end of the launch show I watched a playback of our rehearsals, and when we started we were all tripping up over ourselves and now we are actually doing a routine. It's amazing.'

The 34-year-old singer has a string of hits to her name, including the top-ten smash 'Superstar', but she insists that doesn't automatically make her a natural dancer.

'People keep saying my musical background will help because we know how to tell a story, but when you're a pop star there is a lot of smoke and mirrors behind you and doing this you realise how lazy you actually were,' she laughs. 'Now I think we had all that opportunity, I should have paid attention to the beats and steps, because I haven't got a clue.'

The mum of two is dancing with Irish pro Tristan MacManus, and when he's not around she can practise her routines at home with dance-crazy daughters Teja, 14, and 10-year-old Tiani. They've been helping her with a few tips already.

'The advice I've been given from my daughters is that I need to remember to stretch. They have been so supportive and excited.'

But Jamelia admits her toughest test will be to keep it together if she gets a mauling from the judges,

'I think it's going to be really difficult for me,' she confesses. 'I'm quite an emotional person and I don't think it will be just with comments about myself, it will be with anyone else too, because we've already got so close. If the judges say anything bad, I will personally take it badly.

'In fact, if Craig says one of his cutting remarks, like, "You dance like a wet sandwich," I'll cry.'

Tristan MacManus

After being the second out of the series last year, with Jennifer Gibney, Tristan is hoping new partner Jamelia can be a Superstar on the dance floor.

'I'm looking forward to this season,' he reveals. 'I think it will be a good one. I'm having a great time working with Jamelia and the best thing is that she really wants to learn. I can't wait to get going.'

The Irish dancer thinks the singer's musical background could prove an advantage.

'An ear for music is always beneficial,' he says. 'Sometimes the hard thing for people is not picking up the steps but how to do it to the music, and the fact that she's worked with a choreographer before might help.'

Tristan started dancing as a child in his home town of Bray, County Wicklow, and competed around Europe, winning many juvenile, junior and amateur titles before dancing professionally on stage. After several seasons on the US *Dancing with the Stars*, partnering the likes of Pamela Anderson and Gladys Knight, he made his debut on the UK show last year.

'My first UK series was great,' he reveals. 'The transition into a show is always interesting but I got lucky with the partner I got in Jennifer. It didn't last too long but I wouldn't have changed anything about it. I had an absolutely great time and I'm still really good friends with her; so I'm delighted that happened and now I'm very excited to get going again.'

For his second *Strictly* outing, he's truely happy to be paired with Jamelia and thinks the Latin dances could be her strength.

'We're doing a waltz first but I'm very excited to work on the Latin stuff with her,' he says. 'Before we worked with each other I assumed she'd be better in the Latin but I genuinely don't know. It's only because I know her music and she does this little dance when she gets excited that's a bit Latin style. But then she wouldn't really do a waltz when she gets excited!'

BACKSTAGE
BILLY

During the week, designer Vicky Gill and her talented team work flat out to get the costumes ready for Saturday. But on the day, she hands the reins to wardrobe supervisor Jane Marcantonio, who runs the well-oiled machine that keeps the couples looking 'fab-u-lous' on the floor. Helping Jane in the busy wardrobe room are Vicky's assistant Esra Gungor, DSI studio manager Theresa Hewlett and several wardrobe assistants, including dressers Billy Kimberley and Stuart Nuttall.

"'Remember, calmness means control" and "Everyone's a winner even though there's only one champion". They are all winners in my eyes.'

Billy has been a backstage fixture since the show began in 2004, keeping the professional dancers and the male celebrities dressed up to the nines.

'I'm a tiny cog in the wheel,' he says modestly. 'When I go in on a Saturday, Vicky has designed the costumes and Jane has the details of what each couple is wearing so we have a briefing, then we check all the outfits, sew mikes in and work out the quick changes.'

During the show Billy stands discreetly off camera, in Claudia's area, giving each couple the once-over before they descend the stairs to perform. 'I check the shirts, see to their shoes and neaten everything up. It's a last-minute technical before they face the world.'

Billy, who trained with The Royal Ballet and Sadler's Wells Theatre before branching out into TV, knows all the tricks of the trade needed on the day.

'If make-up gets on to a cream dress, I know which chemicals to use and what not to use and I carry a little cleaning pack, which has everything I need,' he explains. 'Before the show, we help to stick the stones on belts or shoes, or sew sequins on. Then we help with the quick changes. When it comes to the final, one couple goes on while another couple comes racing off so we only have 2 minutes. I can tie a bow tie in seconds.'

As it's a live show, last-minute adjustments are common.

'We sew ties down so they don't fly up and sew braces on to shirts so they don't fall down. Some dancers have the soles of their shoes scraped and others have oil on their shoes because that makes it slightly sticky, so they don't slip. Ballroom shoes sometimes need Vaseline on the side so that if they catch each other they don't stick.

The Dresser: Billy (centre) with Pasha, wardrobe supervisor Theresa Hewlett (second left) and the wardrobe team.

'We try to think ahead so there are no distractions.'

Competing celebrities are often new to the quick change and that's when Billy's calming influence takes over.

'Through the weeks, I get to know the person and I can talk them through the change and say, "This is what I'm going to start with." If they're nervous I calm them down with my sayings: "Remember, calmness means control" and "Everyone's a winner even though there's only one champion". They are all winners in my eyes.'

Despite their best efforts, the occasional hiccup does occur, but there's little the team can't handle.

'There are often ripped trousers, a button off or a broken zip. I remember one change, towards the final, that was so quick that it needed two of us, so Stuart and I laid the costume out and left it. Then somebody saw it on a chair and thought they'd put it away. Off came the artist for the quick change and no costume!

'Stuart raced around and found the person, grabbed the costume out of his hands and made it back just in time. We didn't tell the artist until afterwards. But that's what live television is all about.'

Jay McGuiness

As one-fifth of The Wanted, Jay McGuiness is used to being a hit on the dance floor. But his actual dancing skills are yet to be revealed.

'We didn't do a lot of moves in The Wanted,' he admits. 'It was more a case of walking round the stage singing and pointing at people. So it was five years of not really doing much.'

However, he hides a twinkle-toed secret that might just help him get to grips with those tricky Latin moves.

'Before the band I went to theatre school, and we did different kinds of dancing, like contemporary dance, so I've had some training. But I'm excited to be learning new dances.'

The Newark-born singer – paired with Aliona Vilani – admits he is nervous about taking the centre stage after being the shy one in the band. But he's Glad He Came.

'When you have four guys it feels like a rabble, and they could go and take over the room so I would join in when I wanted to,' he reveals. 'This does feel different and there's an element of nerves, but I do honestly feel cocooned by a group of lovely people, because all of the other contestants are so friendly. I'm probably on the shy side but they have all made an effort to get to know me, so I do feel looked after.'

Since the band split last year, Jay has been travelling in America and spending time at music festivals, while writing his own material. But his former bandmates – Tom Parker, Max George, Siva Kaneswaran and Nathan Sykes – are thrilled he's putting on his dancing shoes.

'I think they were happy I was coming home and that I was going to be doing something a little bit challenging.'

But what's really worrying the 25-year-old is putting on that party face during the uptempo numbers.

'I think my biggest challenge will be smiling,' he says. 'Not because I'm not happy but because I'm not naturally a smiley person, so when it comes to one of the more enthusiastic dances I think I'm going to really struggle to bring that character out.'

He's not entirely sure about being Strictlified either.

'I think I might go for a few more sequins than I thought I would, but that's *Strictly*,' he laughs. 'You've got to go for it. But I think I'll steer clear of the spray tan.'

That's what they all say.

Aliona Vilani

Strictly's fiery Aliona was delighted to be paired with boy-band star Jay McGuiness. In fact, he was just the guy she Wanted.

'I was so excited and happy,' she reveals. 'He's such a nice guy and I think he's going to learn really well and hopefully improve from week to week. I'm very excited to see what I can make him do and how well he can dance.'

The Russian dancer has some experience of boy-band members, having taken the glitterball trophy in 2011 with McFly's Harry Judd. But she insists the two pupils have little in common other than their musical background.

'Harry and Jay are both quite shy, but they are very different people, and their abilities and how they dance and how they move is very different, so it's hard to compare them.'

In fact, Jay was quaking with nerves on launch night, and Aliona believes his shyness could be the biggest hurdle to overcome. 'Confidence is Jay's number-one problem that he's going to struggle with,' she admits. 'He has low confidence where

dancing is concerned and I think we're going to have to build him up, but hopefully he will get better as the weeks go by. It's not going to happen in one day. The first dances will be very nerve-racking but once he gets the hang of it his confidence will grow.'

Aliona joined *Strictly Come Dancing* in 2009 and took the trophy two years later. But since her triumph with Harry, things haven't been running so smoothly. 'I've been out week one for the past two years,' she laughs. 'Hopefully, Jay will break that curse!'

Jay is proving a fast learner when it comes to the routines but she is taking it one dance step at a time.

'I never think about winning,' she says. 'My main and only concern is to teach Jay so he can reach his potential, and I think he has a lot of potential. But not one pro has ever won twice, a fact I'm trying not to mention to Jay.'

The former champ won't be inviting Jay's pals from The Wanted along to rehearsals either. 'That's never good for the guys,' she explains. 'They just laugh at each other and that's the last thing I want!'

FIT to DANCE

Being a professional dancer means being in peak condition at all times, and that involves healthy living and a whole lot of exercise. *Strictly* pros **Aliona Vilani** and **Kevin Clifton** let us in on the fitness routines and diet secrets that keep them tip-top at all times.

FITNESS

My fitness regime depends on what kind of lifestyle I'm having at that moment.

If I'm not dancing full time, my daily regime includes a cardio session in the gym. I never use weights in any of my exercises, because in my opinion weights make the body look too masculine.

I spend 10 minutes on the cross trainer (my favourite as it works the whole body at the same time), then 10 minutes running, including 2 minutes of fast-paced walking before and after the run to warm up/cool down, and 5 minutes on the

bike. I believe that it's better to do less but more often than more and less often, so every weekday is ideal with a day or two off.

I finish with a 45-minute stretching and strengthening routine which I have developed myself over the years, to condition my body. It consists of exercises from my early years of ballet warm-up classes, some moves based on yoga classes and gymnastics and some basic Latin and ballroom moves that include isolations. Combined, they make a great routine that stretches, strengthens and tones your whole body. If used daily, it creates great, healthy results.

If I'm working, I skip cardio, as I get that from dancing, so I just do my strengthening routine.

HEALTHY EATING

I like to have a balanced diet and a little bit of everything is good.

I love to drink herbal teas like jasmine, fruit tea, green tea and my favourites, mint tea with honey or camomile tea with brown sugar. I rarely drink coffee but I will have a caffè latte after a meal if I'm eating out.

I do love my desserts and chocolates, which I have almost daily with tea, but the key for me is very small portions. I try to make different freshly squeezed juices as often as I can at home.

DAILY MENU

For breakfast I alternate the following:
1. Two-egg omelette with avocado, tomatoes, orange pepper, ham and fresh parsley. (See page 74)
2. Rice pudding with fresh berries.
3. Scrambled or poached eggs with smoked salmon and a tomato, avocado and wild-rocket salad on the side.
4. Vanilla yogurt with fresh fruit and granola.
5. Two fried eggs with one sausage, one rasher of bacon and tomatoes. (My husband's speciality.)

For lunch my ideal meal would be seafood or chicken salad.

In the evening I'll have fish, chicken or meat, with a side of potato, served various ways, and occasionally pasta. I always have some kind of small salad, vegetables or greens like beans, spinach or broccoli.

Kevin

FITNESS

Before I launch into the ins and outs of how I look after myself in terms of fitness, let's make one thing clear: I HATE the gym! I get very bored in a gym.

The great thing about being a dancer is that it is possibly the best kind of cardio workout you can get. So when I'm dancing a lot I don't need the gym as it's working my muscles, core and general fitness levels with the added bonus of doing something I love.

Throughout *Strictly Come Dancing*, the pros are often dancing between 8 and 12 hours a day for close to five months. This is more than enough 'fitness training' and, as far as food is concerned, I can pretty much eat whatever I want.

The danger comes after *Strictly* has finished. At this point the body has adapted to dancing all day, every day and suddenly it isn't doing that any more so it's easy to put on weight and lose fitness levels.

The key for me is to trick my brain into thinking I'm having fun (like when I'm dancing) as opposed to working. I'm a big sports fan and love boxing so I take private boxing lessons for fitness. If anyone has ever tried this they'll appreciate the intense fitness needed by boxers just to get through one round, let alone 12!

If I can't get to a boxing class then there's no alternative. Back to the gym!

This time the key to tricking my mind into thinking I'm having a great time is a playlist of my favourite music pumping through my headphones.

I've never had the muscular physique of a WWE wrestler and I'm not sure it's particularly ideal for a dancer, but I do lift some weights. It's best to alternate different muscle groups on different days, so I work on shoulders, chest and triceps one day, back and biceps on another and legs and abs on another. I usually begin my workout with half an hour on the treadmill but rather than a long jog I do interval training, alternating between 1 minute of walking and 1 minute of sprinting. It's great for attacking fat and means I can still tuck into some tasty treats.

HEALTHY EATING

When it comes to food, I never really stick to a strict diet: my wife Karen is far too good a cook for that! She loves trying out new recipes and I am more than happy to be her guinea pig. In general, though, we tend to eat healthily at home. If we are preparing for *Strictly* or one of our own shows, we will cut out snacks such as chocolate, crisps and sweets, and also alcohol. It's good to eat plenty but eat healthy.

Aliona's Breakfast Omelette with Rocket, Tomato and Avocado Salad

Serves one

Ingredients
- 2 eggs
- A drop of milk
- 3 cherry tomatoes, cut in half
- ¼ orange pepper, cut into chunky slices
- ½ avocado, stoned, peeled and cut into chunky slices (use the other half for the salad)
- 1 slice of ham, cut into small strips
- Handful of fresh parsley, roughly chopped
- 1 teaspoon of butter
- Sea salt and freshly ground black pepper

Salad
- A handful of wild rocket leaves
- 3 cherry tomatoes, cut in half
- ½ avocado, stoned, peeled and cut into chunky slices
- 1 teaspoon of virgin olive oil
- 1 teaspoon of balsamic vinegar
- Sea salt and freshly ground black pepper

---

1. Whisk the eggs and milk in a bowl until combined. Add the tomatoes, pepper, avocado, ham and parsley, and swirl until all the ingredients are covered with egg. Season with salt and black pepper.

2. Heat the butter in a small frying pan over a medium heat. Swirl the butter round to cover the entire pan, including the sides, so that the omelette doesn't stick.

3. Turn down the heat to low.

4. Pour all the ingredients into the pan, spread evenly and cover with a lid, occasionally uncovering to let it breathe. Cook for about 5 minutes or until the top of the omelette is firm.

5. Once the omelette is done, slide it on to a plate and top it with the wild-rocket leaves, cherry tomatoes and avocado. Drizzle with virgin olive oil and balsamic vinegar, then sprinkle with sea salt and black pepper.

Kevin's
Roasted Salmon
with Avocado
& Quinoa Salad
Serves one

This is one of my favourite
healthy 'Karen Specials'.

Ingredients
- 1 salmon fillet
- 1 teaspoon of extra virgin olive oil
- 85g of quinoa
- 1 ripe avocado
- 1 lime
- Salt and pepper

---

1. Pre-heat the oven to 200°C.

2. Season the salmon with a little salt and
pepper and rub with the olive oil.

3. Roast on a foil-lined baking sheet
for about 20 minutes.

4. Cook the quinoa with 225ml of salted
boiling water for 12 minutes. Make sure
all the water is absorbed.

5. Dice the avocado into bite-sized pieces.

6. Once the salmon is cooked,
serve on a plate with the quinoa
and avocado, and finish with a
squeeze of lime and some
salt and pepper to taste.

Bon appétit!

Anita Rani

Broadcaster Anita has made one member of her family very happy by signing up to strut her stuff on the dance floor.

'I'm basically living out my mother's dream,' she reveals. 'She came from India to marry my dad and she used to watch the original *Come Dancing* when she was pregnant with me. She told me, "This is what I always imagined I wanted to do when I came to England – wear ballroom dresses and dance." So no pressure for me then.'

The *Countryfile* host is often found in jeans and wellies, and she admits those skimpy Latin numbers are not her natural look.

'The outfits are going to be a challenge,' she says. 'I'm way out of my comfort zone with them. The dress for the launch show was almost like the costume department had a massive joke with me. It's like they've said, "Who's going to be the most terrified of exposing herself?"'

The 37-year-old presenter says she is 'superexcited' to be paired with new dancer Gleb Savchenko and jokes about his legendary good looks: 'I don't know if he can teach me to dance because I can't actually look at his face.'

A huge *Strictly* fan, Anita has been swotting up on past winners to pick up some tips for her own dances.

'I have watched everything,' she says. 'I'm obsessed with *Strictly* so I've watched all the old dances with Caroline Flack and Kara Tointon. It's terrifying. But I just want to learn how to dance. I love the Latin numbers, the supersexy ones, the things I've never done in my life. That's what I'm looking forward to the most.'

Anita couldn't wait to meet the professionals and the other contestants – and got overexcited about one lady in particular.

'Because we're all so terrified and we're all in the same boat, we've all just clung to each other straight away,' she said. 'I sort of knew I loved Jamelia before I met her and when I did I sort of threw myself at her and said, "I love you!" Luckily she loves me too – or so she said!'

Gleb Savchenko

Russian star Gleb is new to *Strictly* in the UK, but he's a familiar sight to judges Len and Bruno, as a professional on *Dancing with the Stars* in the US. The globetrotting dancer has also worked on the shows in his home country and Australia before coming to the UK.

'I'm excited to be joining the British show,' he reveals. 'It's the best in the world.'

Dancing with *Countryfile* presenter Anita Rani, Gleb believes he could make quite an impact in his debut year.

'I was very happy to be paired with Anita,' he says. 'She's got a great personality, she's funny, she's got a lot of potential. Most importantly she is willing to put in a lot of hard work and a lot of time, and that's what I like.

'I think she's going to be great in both Latin and ballroom. She has a natural rhythm in the body and she feels it. She has good coordination.'

The *Countryfile* star will need to muck in if she's going to keep her tutor happy.

'I would say I'm patient but I'm tough,' he reveals. 'I like to work hard.'

Gorgeous Gleb, who has also modelled for major brands and danced with Jennifer Lopez, is guaranteed to set pulses racing around the country. But he is a family man, happily married to fellow dancer Elena Samodanova and dad to 4-year-old daughter Olivia, whom he calls 'the cutest thing in the world'.

'We have homes in Sydney, LA and Hong Kong, so this season I'm here on my own while my wife and daughter are in Hong Kong, but they're going to come and visit whenever they can.'

Born in Moscow, Gleb started dancing at 8 and has competed in Latin contests around the world, dancing with Elena for ten years before they both appeared on *Dancing with the Stars* in Australia. Elena now judges on the Russian version, where Gleb danced with Olympic figure skater Adelina Sotnikova earlier this year.

'My wife judged me last season in Russia,' he laughs. 'And she was very tough on me!'

Craig should be a doddle then.

Craig does his own make-up for the show, so he keeps his bag of tricks on his dressing table. 'I have eyelash curlers, nasal-hair trimmers, foundation and brushes,' he says. 'Plus plenty of water to keep me hydrated.'

The Judge's Chamber

Deep in the heart of Elstree Studios, tucked away from the bustle of the *Strictly* stage, is a long corridor of doors, each marked with a glitterball and a familiar name. Behind these hallowed doors lie the dressing rooms of presenters Tess and Claudia, the fabulous guest stars and, of course, all four judges. This inner sanctum is the fearsome foursome's haven of peace before the excitement of the live show, where they glam up for the bright lights and prep themselves to take centre stage and deliver their verdicts on the evening's effort.

Now, in a *Strictly*-confidential first, judge Craig Revel Horwood has opened his doors to his own dressing room to give us a sneak peak at his Saturday hang-out.

'I get here about one o'clock then meet and greet the other judges, and we film video inserts for the show. Then we go to the studio and have a meeting with choreographer Jason Gilkison to learn our opening routines, which we don't know until the day.

'After lunch, I write my book up, which means I write down the order of the contestants and the judges' speaking order, then we have an hour off before we go live.'

After the show, Craig nips back to the dressing room before joining the dancers and guests in the pay bar. 'I leave about midnight and head home to my house in Hampshire, and I generally get in about two in the morning.'

A fridge is provided for drinks and food, and a kettle sits on top for tea and coffee. It's a long day for the judges, so Craig has healthy snacks on hand to get him through.

'I must have lean cooked chicken plus water, Diet Coke, two bags of peanuts, two bananas and two apples.'

Iwan Thomas

Sprinter Iwan has cabinets heaving with medals from the Olympics and the World Athletics Championships, and he's got his eye on the prize once more with *Strictly*. He's hoping his competitive nature will be the key to unlocking his dancing potential.

'I think we pick things up quickly as sportsmen and we don't like to be rubbish at anything,' he explains. 'I did *MasterChef* a couple of years ago, and I was terrible but I ended up as runner-up because I don't like to lose so I worked at it. When I came to *Strictly* I thought I was going to be bad, but within a few days I picked up quite a lot.

'I'm not saying I'm a great dancer but I'm determined to be better than where I start.'

The 400-metres champ is hoping to be in for the long haul this time, but is worried that the judges' criticisms might trip him up.

'Constructive criticism is a good thing, but I'm quite a sensitive bloke and I don't like being told off,' he says. 'When I do get told I'm rubbish, which I will be, I'll have to take it on the chin rather than fight back.'

Although he's had his fair share of challenges, the 41-year-old sportsman believes dancing is a world away from running.

'As an athlete, everything is clear cut. I just had to get from A to B as fast as I could and the stopwatch doesn't lie. If I've run slowly, it's there in black and white. However this is very subjective and someone might just not like the way you dance. I could think I've really nailed a dance and Craig or someone else might say I didn't. So I've got to take technical criticism, which I've never had. That's tough.'

To get him through, Iwan has the help of former champ Ola Jordan, but he admits she's got her work cut out.

'Ola will have to be very patient because my concentration is not great,' he says. 'I need someone to be kind and considerate rather than cracking the whip.'

Swapping the Lycra for the sparkles and sequins hasn't been a problem for Iwan.

'I'm loving the outfits,' he says, grinning. 'I want more glitter and tighter tops. I have asked if I can reveal a lot more by week 3 or 4. I'm the campest straight bloke you'll ever see on *Strictly*.'

Ola Jordan

Seasoned pro Ola might have trouble giving her celeb partner the runaround this year. Iwan Thomas is a record-breaking Olympic sprinter so he should have no problem with the faster routines.

'He's a sportsman so he works hard in the studio,' says Ola. 'I always like working with sports people because they are focused; they're really good. They have the right mentality and on the live show they tend to put on a good performance. But it's too early to say whether he will dance well. Iwan has never danced before and we just have to take it slowly and get there somehow.'

What he lacks in experience he makes up for in enthusiasm, though, and even with Ola cracking the whip, he can be a tad naughty.

'He's a bit like an excited little boy all the time, which is nice because he jokes around a lot, so he's fun to work with,' she laughs. 'He's very enthusiastic, very positive and it's lovely to have someone like that in the training room.'

Ola began dancing at 12 and won the Open Polish Championship at 17, a year before teaming up with future husband James Jordan. The couple turned professional in 2003, the same year they married, and three years later joined the cast of *Strictly Come Dancing*. Series 7 saw her dance her way to victory with sports presenter Chris Hollins, delivering a show-stopping Charleston that remains a *Strictly* classic.

Last year, Ola and *Deadly 60* star Steve Backshall made it to week nine before losing out in the dance off to Sunetra Sarker and Brendan Cole. But Ola says the presenter was very dedicated.

'Steve was lovely and very serious about the show, so everything was focussed on the dance,' she says. 'But he was also very strong, a lot of muscle, so the lifts were great.'

Ola is thrilled that runner Iwan is right on track when it comes to the *Strictly* garb, and she plans to take full advantage.

'Iwan loves the tight outfits, the sparkles and all of that,' she says. 'He is really embracing the whole experience and is throwing himself into it, which is great.

'I've got some great ideas for outfits but I'm not going to give them away. It's a surprise!'

Sew Strictly

Ever fancied adding your own tango twist to your party wardrobe? Break out the needle and thread, because pattern cutter Theresa Hewlett has let us in on a *Strictly* secret, so that you can replicate a skirt worn by tango-queen Flavia Cacace. Happy sewing.

EQUIPMENT NEEDED:
• Wide paper. This can be bought in small quantities from specialist fashion-supply shops, but plain lining wallpaper is also ideal.

• Pencil

• Black marker pen

• Ruler

• Paper scissors

• Fabric scissors

• Dressmaking pins

• Handsewing needle

• Tape measure

• Fabric. Something with a close, even weave is ideal, e.g. cotton, sateen, linen, crêpe, satin-backed crêpe.

• Thread to match your fabric

• Lightweight interfacing/fusing – enough for the waistband.

• Your choice of fastening, e.g. buttons, hooks and eyes, poppers.

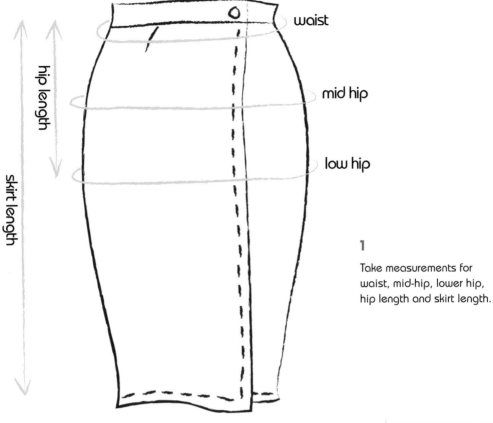

1

Take measurements for waist, mid-hip, lower hip, hip length and skirt length.

	cm	
waist + 4cm		(A)
mid hip + 4cm		(B)
low hip + 4cm		(C)
hip length		(D)
skirt length		(E)

2

Make a measurement chart (see table above). Add 4cm to your measurements, as on the chart, to give the garment 'ease' while wearing.

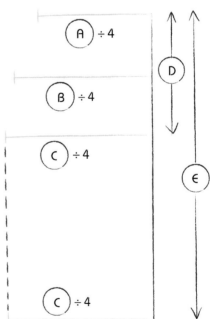

3

For the back skirt:

On the paper, draw a vertical line the length of your skirt and four lines at right angles to match the hip height and length of the skirt; the length of these lines should be a quarter of the measurements from your chart.

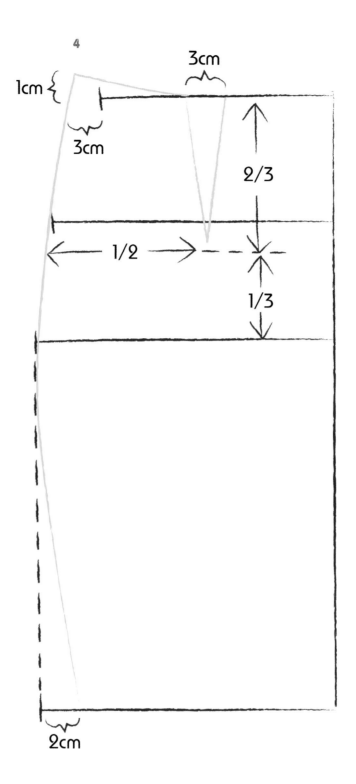

4 Draw in the side seam and mark a back dart. (A back dart is a folded wedge of fabric that is tapered and sewn in order to make the waist measurement smaller than the hip.) To position the dart, follow the proportions of the diagram. The side waist point is moved up by 1cm and away from the centre line by 3cm the waistline is then blended from this point back into the waistline

with a gentle curve. Then the side seam can be drawn in.

The short side of the wedge/triangle should be 3cm for most sizes but can be made larger or smaller depending on body shape.

The two long sides of this triangle are sewn together (right sides of fabric together) and will shape the back skirt into the back waist.

5

6

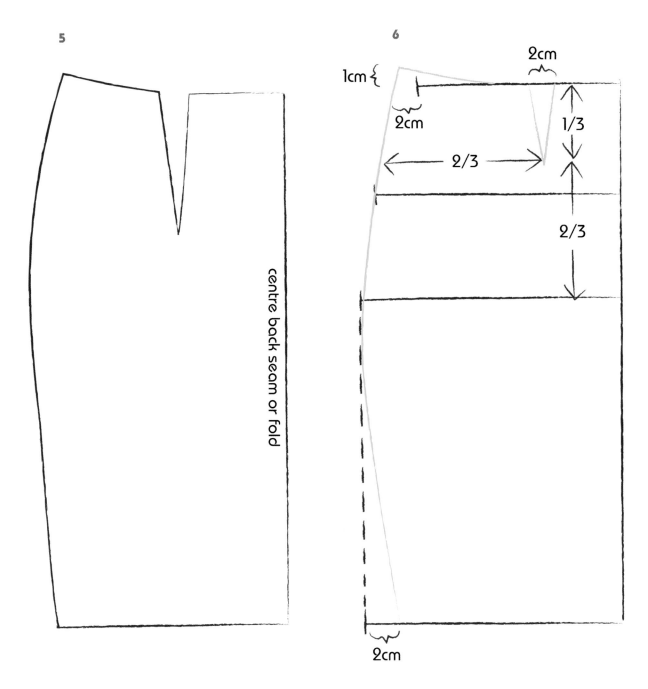

1cm

2cm

2cm

1/3

2/3

2/3

2cm

centre back seam or fold

5 Back pattern. Cut one pair of these with a centre-back seam or cut with the fold of the fabric along the centre-back line.

6 For the front skirt, follow step 3 again and add front darts, with the short side of the triangle measuring 2cm. Move the side waist point and draw in the waistline as on the diagram.

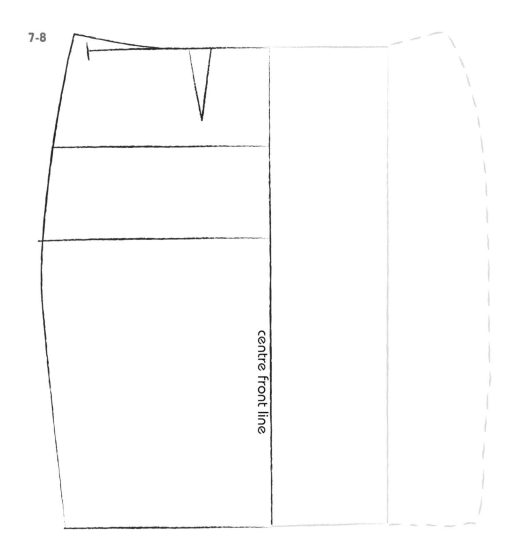

7-8

centre front line

7 Trace through a mirror image of the front skirt from the centre-front line.

To trace the mirror image through from the centre-front line, fold the paper along the centre-front line, so that there is a layer of paper over the front pattern you have just drawn. Be careful to fold the paper exactly on the centre-front line or the skirt will end up the wrong size. The paper should be transparent enough to be able to see the pattern marking through the top layer (you may have to mark the original pattern marks in thick black pen if it is difficult to see through). Trace through the pattern markings on to the blank overlay of paper. Fold out the paper so that you have a 'double' front pattern.

At this stage each half of the pattern will be drawn on one side of the paper and half on the other. Trace through one half of the pattern so that you have a whole front-skirt pattern.

Alternatively, if your paper is opaque, you can mark and cut out two front patterns and tape them together at the centre-front line to give you a whole front pattern.

8 Choose wrap width and draw a vertical line from this point. The wrap width is a personal choice, but we would suggest a classic measurement, which is the distance from the centre-front to the hip bone. Once the front pattern is finished, you will need to cut one pair of fronts.

9 Add seam allowances. This depends on the fabric, but an average is 1.5cm for a non-stretch fabric. An average hem length is 4cm.

The waistband width is your own preference, although Flavia's skirt would have had a 2.5cm band.

To make a 2.5cm band, draw a rectangle twice the width of the band (5cm) and a length of the total waist measurement of the skirt (left-front waist including wrap + right-front waist including wrap + total back waist). Measure with the darts already sewn.

Add a seam allowance of 1.5cm all round. You will need to trim the seams of the band down after sewing to reduce any bulk.

10 Sew the skirt together and add the waistband before fitting to determine exactly how much the fronts should overlap.

To add a waistband, follow the instructions below:
Before sewing the waistband, if your fabric is light, stabilise the waistband by ironing some fusible interfacing on to the wrong side of the fabric. This will make the waistband firmer and easier to work with, plus it will wear better.

The vertical edges of the skirt need to be sewn/hemmed before stitching on the waistband.

Once the vertical edges of the skirt have been finished, pin one of the long sides of the waistband along the waistline of the skirt, right sides together.

Sew along the waistband, making an even line parallel to the raw edges, the width of the seam allowance. Trim the seam allowance to about half its width.

Fold the waistband in half along the length of the band, right sides together, and pin (it should look like it is inside out at this stage).

At each end of the waistband, with the bulk of the main skirt facing you, right sides up, fold up the remaining seam allowance on the unsewn side of the waistband and pin. Do this for only 3cm from the end of the waistband.

Sew across the end of the waistband, along the seam line, parallel to the raw edge and at right angles to the first waistband seam line. (You should be sewing on the wrong side of the fabric.) Trim the seam allowances to about half their width.

Remove the pins and 'turn out' (turn the sewn piece through so that the right sides are uppermost, and the seams are now on the inside) the end of the waistband. These should now be square with the seam allowance inside.

Press the waistband, folding in the remaining seam on the underside of the band as you go.

Slip-stitch along the inner side of the waistband to hold it all together.

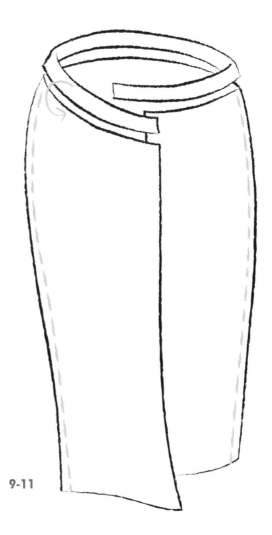

9-11

Slip-stitch is a handsewing stitch. A few threads of the fabric should be picked up with the needle from one side of the two edges that need to be sewn. Then, about 0.5cm along, pick up a few threads from the other side, then another 0.5cm along, a few from the original side. Carry on like this, taking a few threads from each side and pulling the threaded needle through them in turn, until the waistband is sewn along its length.

When the overlap has been marked, the waistband can be fastened with either a hook and eye, poppers or machined buttonholes.

A fastening should be applied to each 'end' of the waistband, so one set of fastenings will be underneath the waistband, hidden from view, to stop the 'under wrap' from falling down when it is worn.

The hooks and eyes or poppers are handsewn, but the buttonhole is sewn using the buttonhole feature on your sewing machine.

Kellie Bright

The queen of the Queen Vic is swapping Walford for the waltz as she hits a landmark birthday.

'I'm going to be 40 soon and I thought this was a good time to get the fittest I've ever been in my life,' she admits. 'How amazing to learn how to dance like that and to be whizzed around the dance floor. The little girl in me can't wait.'

The *EastEnders* star – who is partnered by Kevin Clifton – is worried about the graceful ballroom routines but is up for a good time in all the dances.

'I'm quite into the jive, because it's bouncy and fun,' she reveals. 'The trouble with the ballroom is that it's so elegant and poised, and I don't think I'm a naturally poised person. So I might struggle with the technique.

'But I'm determined to have fun. The people I've enjoyed watching over the years are the ones where you can just see the joy. I loved watching Alison Hammond last year because she was just having the time of her life and you could see it.'

Essex-born Kellie, who stars as landlady Linda Carter in the soap, says being herself instead of a character is 'the scariest thing'.

'It's like crossing a line,' she says. 'I'm going to think of myself as a character who is a dancer. That's how I'm going to approach it. So whenever I'm on the dance floor I'm not me, I'm a dancer.'

As one of the soap's leading stars, Kellie will still be filming intense storylines between training sessions and, with a 3-year-old son at home, her schedule is pretty full. But fellow *EastEnders* Jake Wood has been on hand to help.

'Jake told me to "sleep and eat". But it's learning my lines that worries me. It's one thing having to film all day and then rehearse in the evening, but when do I learn the lines? I only have Sunday and I have to spend a little bit of time with my family otherwise my son will forget who I am.'

As well as Jake and former *Strictly* star Scott Maslen, the Albert Square actress has screen husband Danny Dyer backing her bid for the glitterball trophy, and she says he 'couldn't be more supportive'.

'He was quite nervous for me,' she says. 'I think it's the live-show element. But he's excited for me. He's also a bit jealous I'm going to be dancing with someone else day in, day out. I said, "You're not even my real husband!"'

Kevin Clifton

Every series of *Strictly* holds magic moments for the pro dancers, but newly-wed Kevin, who tied the knot with Karen Hauer in July, is looking forward to one very specific aspect of the live shows.

'I can't wait to hear the voiceover announce, "Now, Jeremy Vine and Karen Clifton ..." That will be a special moment.'

While he's happy to pull off a live performance every Saturday night, the Grimsby lad admits he was a bag of nerves when it came to the couple's big day.

'It was an amazing day,' he reveals. 'But I was really nervous. I don't know why. We're so used to performing in front of millions of people on *Strictly* and then all of a sudden all these eyes were on me, my closest family and friends, and I wasn't there to dance! I was an emotional wreck.'

Back for his third year on *Strictly*, Kevin says he is already having a ball with his partner, *EastEnders* star Kellie Bright.

'It can be awkward in those first stages when you're getting to know each other,' he says. 'But Kellie is so full of life, enthusiastic and a good laugh, so we clicked straight away.'

But can he hold on to his record of never being in a dance-off?

'Kellie's not a dancer so it's not natural to her, but she really listens and she's a bit of a perfectionist. She really works at it. If she carries on applying herself like that, she should be really good.'

Last year, Kevin made the finals for the second year running, with singer Frankie Bridge.

'Frankie was great,' he recalls. 'She could pick up the steps easily, but she was quite shy about being a performer and I think she was used to having four girls around her in The Saturdays. We did a lot of work on the character of each dance, acting it out, whereas, as an actress, that should be easier for Kellie and we'll have to work more on the dance side.

'I'm going to try and tap into the acting and give her a character and a script for each dance, so she can perform to the dance as much as possible.'

Kevin is also looking forward to dancing around Albert Square and meeting Kellie's screen hubby.

'I don't watch many soaps,' he laughs. 'I'm more of a *Match of the Day* man! But I'm hoping to get on set. I want to hang out with Danny Dyer.'

TAN-TASTIC

Strictly **is not just about going for gold. Sometimes it's all about the bronze. And those gorgeous bodies just wouldn't look the same without the sunkissed finish courtesy of fake-tan supremo Jules Heptonstall.**

Every Friday, straight after the dress rehearsals, the celebrities make their way to two booths backstage at Elstree Studios. There wait Jules Heptonstall and his assistant, spray guns loaded and ready.

'We are the last thing they do on rehearsal days,' explains Jules. 'They come straight from rehearsals, have a shower and a tan, then get in a onesie and go to dinner.

'They are given special tanning onesies and we give them a tan-care kit, with aloe-vera body butter and exfoliators. We need them to exfoliate the last tan off so the next one looks good.'

The spray gun is not the only trick Jules uses to make the male dancers look their best.

'If the boys have their chests out, we contour their torso with extra tan and make them look super-defined. It's like we're painting on muscles. Backstage secret!'

Some of the younger celebs, particularly singers and presenters, are used to spray tans but others are nervous when they first face the booth.

'Guys are quite shy about having tans, but once they see the results, they want it,' says Jules. 'Last year, Mark Wright tried to resist, which surprised us because he's the most Essex boy around. But often they start saying, "I don't want one," and once they've had it, they say, "This is amazing."

'Part of being a good spray tanner is making someone feel comfortable in the booth. Once they relax, everybody enjoys being pampered. In the

first week, each person takes 45 minutes, because they don't know me, they need to get comfortable, and it's all very new. By the end of the series it takes 15 minutes.'

Jules uses an 'intelligent tan' that reacts to the skin tone to create the perfect shade and develops overnight. It's then showered off so it won't mark the costumes.

'We make bespoke tans as some people like their legs or back darker. It's all about the distance you hold the gun from the body, the speed you move at, and the solution that's in the gun.'

The bronzed look is more than an aesthetic change. It evens skin tone, covers signs of fatigue and provides the oft-needed confidence boost.

'Often they are nervous about their dance, or their costumes. People think celebrities are superhuman, but they still have their body issues, so a tan gives them a boost.

'It's the first part of preparing for Saturday, because once that tan goes on it's like something switches in their mind and they're in show mode.

'The bright colours on the dance floor, along with the glaring TV lights, can make people look quite grey, so the tan is important. It's all part of Strictlification.'

As with the costumes, the shade of tan depends on the dance being performed.

'For something like the waltz we keep it really light but if they're doing the rumba, or the paso doble, we use a dark tan to reflect the drama of the dance.

Ballroom Bitz

Dazzle fellow fans with your
in-depth *Strictly Come Dancing* knowledge.
Here are some fun facts and stats to get
under your spangled belt.

The total number of perfect 10s awarded by the judges in the main series is 477. Although Darcey has only been a full-time judge for three series, she has already awarded more perfect scores than Craig, with a total of 58 to his 40. Bruno has awarded 160 and Len 127.

The judges '1' paddle has only been raised nine times – and eight of those were by Craig.

Caroline Flack holds the record for the most maximum scores in a series, with four. She also has the most consecutive perfect scores, having bagged a 40 in the semi-final and three in the final.

For each series, an average of 1.5 million fans apply for tickets to watch the live shows, which are allocated on a lottery system.

Artem Chigvintsev holds the record for most Botafogos in 30 seconds after performing 79 on *It Takes Two* in 2011.

Frank Sinatra is the most played artist on the show, with 27 of his famous songs providing the backdrop for the competitive routines so far. Michael Bublé is second with 21 and Robbie Williams has notched up 19.

Ola Jordan holds the record for hair extensions. She had three sets weighing 4.5kg in total for the Halloween special in 2011.

If you want to be a record breaker, the samba and the rumba are the ones to go for. They are the only dances that have yet to get a perfect score, with top marks of 39 so far.

Kicking off the show is no bad thing. Of the 12 celebrities who have danced first, four have won and two more have been runners-up. The winners are Natasha Kaplinsky, Darren Gough, Tom Chambers and Caroline Flack. Matt Dawson and Matt Di Angelo narrowly missed out on the trophy after starting the series.

All the winners have been in their 20s or 30s. The oldest was Chris Hollins, at 38, and the youngest was Louis Smith, at 23.

For each series, an average of 504 cans of hairspray is used. That's 252 litres, enough to fill a very large bath or six Mini Cooper petrol tanks. More than 200 rollers and hot sticks are used for each show, and about four hairdryers blow up each year.

Peter Andre

Singer Peter may be ready to face the fearsome foursome on the judging panel but his harshest critics are likely to be at home. The dad of three is under strict instructions from 10-year-old Junior and 8-year-old Princess not to make a fool of himself.

'They said to me, "You embarrass us, just once, don't come home!"' he laughs. 'But they are fans of the show and they do want to come and watch. Princess wants to try on all the outfits, of course, and Junior wants to meet all the dancers. He's a bit of a cheeky one.'

The Aussie entertainer, coupled with Janette Manrara, has had to bust a few moves in pop videos, most notably for his smash hit 'Mysterious Girl'. But he thinks the judges' criticism could help him in his future performances.

'The judges on this show know their stuff,' he says. 'So if Craig tells me to keep my thumbs in, because apparently Craig doesn't like thumbs, I'll take that on board.'

Despite his famous six-pack, shy Peter is not in a rush to go for the full Latin look.

'The more the girls try on the outfits the more excited they get,' he says. 'But the outfits did freak me out at first, as they told me they would, but they also said that by mid-series I would be asking for more diamanté, more bling and the rest.'

The 42-year-old admits to a competitive streak but says his main aim is to push himself to the limits.

'People ask if I want to be better than one person or another but the other day I read a saying that was spot on: "You don't want to be better than anyone else, you want to be better than yourself." I love that because you get in this zone and you aren't looking at anyone else. You need to focus.'

Away from *Strictly*, he's not keen on his dancing taking centre stage – even at his wedding. The singer tied the knot with fiancée Emily in July, and they chose Eva Cassidy's 'Songbird' as their first dance.

'It was just a smoochy dance and halfway through I whispered, "Are you over this?" and Emily said, "I'm SO over this." We couldn't wait to get through it.'

He may be feeling the same when those Saturday-night nerves kick in.

Janette Manrara

Janette has plenty to celebrate as she embarks on her third series of *Strictly*. Not only has she bagged singer Peter Andre as her dance partner, she recently got engaged to the show's very own Aljaž.

'It all came as a big surprise to me,' she reveals. 'We haven't set a wedding date because right now the priority is to work on this series and get our partners looking as good as we can. Once the series is done we'll start thinking about the wedding.'

The American dancer is 'thrilled' to be partnering Peter because 'he's so sweet, so friendly and, on top of that, he's talented'. And she thinks his musical background will help when it comes to wowing the judges.

'I've only seen his music videos and the group rehearsals but he looks like he has a lot of potential,' she says.

'His strength is the fact that he is a performer and he seems to be quite passionate about dancing and music. He's a big powerhouse so he might struggle a little bit with the softer, more romantic dances, but we'll see.'

The downside, says Janette, is that expectations are high. 'I think Peter feels a lot of pressure because everyone expects him to do so well, so I don't want to put pressure on him. Obviously the eyes are on the prize but we are going to take it one dance at a time.'

While his female fans will be hoping for a glimpse of that famous six-pack, Janette says 'He's actually quite shy,' she reveals. 'So he wants to feel 100 per cent confident and I'm going to give him time and let him choose if he wants to.'

Janette, who joined the show in 2013, reached the semi-finals last year with *EastEnders*'s Jake Wood.

'It was an incredible year for me,' she recalls. 'Jake and I are still really good friends and I love his wife and kids, so Aljaž and I go over for dinner.

'Jake is a true example of what *Strictly* is all about. He'd never danced, never done music videos or anything like that and he came out and did so well. To be on that journey with him was wonderful.'

The actor's week 2 salsa proved one of the most memorable dances of the season, with Bruno dubbing it 'undiluted full-on fantastic!'

'I haven't decided how I'm going to top that with Peter,' laughs Janette. 'But I'll feel a bit of pressure when the salsa comes on.'

STRICTLY FAQS

How many dances allow lifts?

Three lifts are now permitted in the American Smooth and unlimited lifts in the showdance. Lifts are also allowed in the Charleston, Argentine tango and the salsa. A lift is any move in which both feet leave the floor at the same time.

Which celeb has scored the highest judges' scores in a series?

Ricky Whittle has the highest total score, with a whopping 766 for 19 dances and the highest average of 40.3 which includes extra points from series seven guest judge Darcey. Without those, Natalie Gumede tops the leader board for average score, with 553 points for 15 dances, which works out at an average of 36.9. A tough act to beat – even though she lost out on the trophy to Abbey Clancy.

How does the scoring system work?

The couples are first ranked according to the combined judges' scores and the couple with the highest score are awarded points equal to the number of competing pairs. For example, if 15 couples are competing in show one, then the top scorers will earn 15 points and the lowest scorers will get one point.

Viewers then log their own votes by phone and online. After these are counted and verified, the couples are again ranked, this time according to the number of votes received. The couple with the highest ranking is then awarded the number of points equal to the competing couples on the night in descending order, as before.

The two scores are then added together to determine who will be in the bottom two and facing elimination. The system ensures that even those with the highest judges' scores can find themselves in the bottom two.

What happens if there is a tie?

If two or more couples have the same points, once the judges' scores and viewers' votes have been combined, the couple with the highest number of viewer votes will be placed ahead on the leader board.

Do the judges make notes during the performances?

Each judge has a notepad and pencil on the judges' desk in case they want to make notes during the dance. They may scribble down a word or two, to remind them of something they have spotted during the routine.

How many dresses are made for each series and how much to do they cost?

This series there will be 764 costumes in total and half of those are for the ladies.

Most of the dresses are actually rented, so the cost to the BBC is about £300 per dress on dresses these can then be re-hired and recycled after the UK show has aired. The cost iof making it from scratch, if sold our right to the BBC, would be up to £1500.

Is it really only at the launch show that the pros and celebrities find out who they're paired with?

Yes, the pairing is top secret and decided late in the process. Sometimes the pros and celebs are even changed around the day the launch show is recorded.

As Strictly is broadcast live is there a plan for if something unexpected happens?

The BBC thoroughly researches contingencies to cover all sorts of situations and employs a specific contingency producers over the weekend when the show's being filmed. You have to think on your toes for a live show!

Kirsty Gallacher

Well-connected Kirsty has the backing of some *Strictly* superstars as she takes her first steps – with last year's winner and the show's only competing couple in her corner.

'Caroline Flack is a friend of mine and she said the whole experience is an adventure and life-changing,' she reveals. 'Gabby and Kenny Logan also said, "It's such a great journey, you have got to be a part of it and you will love it."'

The sports presenter will be put through her paces by Brendan Cole and is already in peak physical condition. But she's not sure that gives her much of an advantage.

'The only way it helps is that you have a bit of cardio fitness and maybe a bit of core strength, which might help when I'm being spun round or dragged behind. But having that fitness means nothing really. You still need to get your feet moving the right way and remember your moves!'

But it might help when it comes to her biggest dance-floor fear. 'I'm scared of the jive and anything with complex footwork,' she reveals. 'Anything that I have to move really fast in is going to be a challenge.'

As well as learning the routines, the 39-year-old Sky Sports journalist will have to adjust to having the spotlight turned on her after years of grilling sporting legends.

'Last week when we were filming and they were asking me lots of questions, I was thinking, This is so embarrassing! I usually ask the questions,' she laughs. 'I don't talk about myself, so that is a bit cringe.'

The competitive presenter isn't going to take too kindly to any bad comments from the judges' desk either.

'I'm going to have to bite my tongue because I'm not very good at taking criticism,' she admits. 'But it's what they do, and having watched *Strictly* for years I know that nobody ever gets off scot-free. It wouldn't be *Strictly* if there wasn't a bit of "dis-ah-ster, darling".'

Brendan Cole

*S*trictly stalwart Brendan is known for his tough training regime but this time he has landed himself a pretty sporty model in Kirsty Gallacher. The superfit Sky Sports presenter likes to push herself physically and already has victory on the TV show *The Games* under her belt.

'I'm really excited for the new series and delighted with the partnership,' says Brendan, beaming. 'I'm chuffed to bits to get Kirsty. In terms of training it's early days but so far the rehearsals are going really well. We are both having a great time getting to know each other and working hard.'

One of two original pros, along with Anton Du Beke, the lofty New Zealander was the first to lift the glitterball trophy, in series 1, with Natasha Kaplinsky. Since then he has partnered the likes of Kelly Brook, Lisa Snowdon, Sophie Ellis-Bextor and Claire King, and he's danced in three grand finals.

Now he's hoping Kirsty's love of sports will take him all the way to the Final once again.

'It's too early to see her full potential but she comes from a sports background, she has a great attitude and she's very determined. These are just the qualities you need to be able to succeed.'

Brendan started dancing at the age of 6, following in the footsteps of dancing siblings Scott and Vanessa. In 1996, he began dancing with Camilla Dallerup, turning professional four years later and becoming the New Zealand and Asian Open Professional Dance Champions. They also made the semi-finals at the International, UK Open, British Open and World Dance Championships.

As well as competing in *Strictly*, Brendan has been a judge on New Zealand's *Dancing with the Stars*, alongside arch nemesis Craig Revel Horwood.

Brendan's known as a bit of a Strictly 'bad boy' but he has softened up a bit in recent years. But will this year's competition bring out the fiery side once again?

We will have to wait and see.

STRICTLY QUIZ

So you think you're on the ball when it comes to ballroom?
In the loop about Latin?
Test your *Strictly Come Dancing* knowledge with our fun quiz.

1.
Which contestant was the recipient of
guest judge Donny Osmond's
generous 10 in series 12?

2.
Champs Kara Tointon and Jill Halfpenny have
both appeared in which TV soap?

3.
Bruno Tonioli hails from which
European country?

4.
Zoe Ball danced in series 3 of the
show, but who was her partner?

5.
Name the voice who introduces
the couple's dance.

6.
Which judge has directed the *Strictly
Come Dancing* live tour since 2011?

7.
To which Take That song did series 10 winner
Louis Smith perform his showdance?

8.
Who was the first celebrity
to bag a perfect score?

9.
Frankie Bridge competed in the
last series, but which of her
Saturdays bandmates danced on
the 2013 Christmas special?

10.
Who did Craig Revel Horwood dub
a 'lobster on acid' after his *Little
Mermaid* samba in series 12?

11.
Which two politicians have
graced the *Strictly* dance floor?

12.
Who was the first celebrity
eliminated in series 11?

13.
What style of dance made
Darcey Bussell a star?

14.
Which dance shares its name
with a city in South Carolina?

15.
Name the Blackpool venue,
famous for its dance competitions,
that provides a special venue for *Strictly*.

Answers: 1. Frankie Bridge, 2. *EastEnders*, 3. Italy, 4. Ian Waite, 5. Alan Dedicoat, 6. Craig Revel Horwood, 7. 'Rule the World', 8. Jill Halfpenny, 9. Rochelle Humes, 10. Scott Mills, 11. Ann Widdecombe and Edwina Currie, 12. Tony Jacklin, 13. Ballet, 14. The Charleston, 15. The Tower Ballroom

CROSSWORD

Across

1. Drummer Harry, *Strictly* champ
2. Surname of singer who lost to Tom Chambers
3. Classic ballroom dance
5. Surname of the show's original male presenter
7. Saucy Latin dance
10. Pro who won first-ever *Strictly* with Natasha Kaplinsky
11. Home of ballroom
12. Surname of series 11 winner
14. Matador dance
15. Pro-dancer Lowe
17. Silver-screen special
20. Ranks the scores on the night
24. Surname of judge Bruno
25. Argentine dance

Down

1. High-energy dance popular in 1950s
2. Final free-for-all
4. Keeps pros and celebs hard at work all week
6. Dance of love
8. Smooth dance
9. Hollywood's dancing legends
13. Len's special number
16. Legal or not
18. Used to show judges' scores
19. High praise from Craig
21. Bottom two go head to head
22. Pro dancer Kristina
23. Surname of series 3 winner

Across: 1. Judd, 2. Stevens, 3. Waltz, 5. Forsyth, 7. Salsa, 10. Brendan Cole, 11. Blackpool, 12. Clancy, 14. Paso doble, 15. Natalie, 17. Movie Week, 20. Leader board, 24. Tonioli, 25. Tango **Down:** 1. Jive, 2. Showdance, 4. Training, 6. Rumba, 8. American, 9. Fred and Ginger, 13. Seven, 16. Lift, 18. Paddle, 19. Fabulous, 21. Dance-off, 22. Rihanoff, 23. Gough

Georgia May Foote

Coronation Street star Georgia is hoping to put her best Foote forward when she twirls on to the floor. Although she has some experience of dancing, from her childhood, she's new to ballroom and Latin.

'I'm going to be a bit rusty for starters so I will be generous and give myself six out of ten so there's room to improve,' she laughs. 'I used to dance when I was younger, and I went to dance school to do hip-hop and street dance, which is massively different from ballroom. I used to freestyle, too, so the more precise and technical dancing is going to be quite difficult.'

The soap star left the cobbles behind her earlier this year and couldn't wait to come into the *Strictly* bubble.

'It's nice to do something completely different and I absolutely love a challenge,' she says. 'I'm so excited. I've been wanting to do this for so long that now it's happening I can't quite believe it.

'I love performing, but to learn something so technical and then be able to take that on into the rest of my life would be lovely.'

The Mancunian actress – known as Katy Armstrong in *Coronation Street* – has the support of former co-star and *Strictly* finalist Natalie Gumede.

'I had a really nice message from her the other day saying, "It's an amazing experience. If you ever need any advice, let me know." That was sweet because I haven't seen her since she left *Coronation Street*. But I don't think people can give you advice. You just have to enjoy yourself.'

The youngest of this year's contestants, at 24, Georgia admits she struggled in the first group rehearsals.

'It was hard work,' she says. 'Everyone came in the second day and couldn't move, and I pulled a muscle in my groin, but it was good fun. The first routine was so fast I literally had the pro dancer dragging me across the floor. I was running to catch up.'

Now paired with newcomer Giovanni Pernice, Georgia says she 'can't wait for the jive' and is getting in the mood with a bit of help from the sparkly costumes.

'The outfits are amazing. As soon as you put them on, you can't stop shimmying everywhere!'

Giovanni Pernice

Newcomer Giovanni certainly means business when it comes to lifting the *Strictly* trophy. He has the words *Nato per vincere*, meaning 'Born to win', tattooed on his wrist alongside the date he won the Italian Dance Championships in 2012. Paired with actress Georgia May Foote, he is sure he has a shot at the title.

'Georgia is an amazing dancer,' he says. 'It's early days but I can just see already that she is a good dancer. I did a very difficult routine for our first jive and she coped incredibly well so I'm really proud of her.

'She's also a nice person; she's great fun. She is exactly what I was hoping for. We will have a lot of good times together. Plus she's short, so she looks up to me, which is good!'

Giovanni first met Georgia at the group rehearsals for the launch show and he was instantly impressed.

'We had a small part together and we had a lot of fun, so I was hoping to get Georgia and then when they paired us I was really happy,' he says. 'And I think she was happy too!'

Born in Palermo, Sicily, Giovanni moved to Bologna at the age of 14 to study dance with some of the best teachers in the world and trained alongside *Strictly*'s very own Joanne Clifton. He is over the moon to be on the show.

'For me it is a dream come true,' he says. 'I'm loving every minute of it.'

The youngest of the male professionals, at 25, he only started learning English in May, before moving to the UK in August.

'The other dancers have made me feel so welcome,' he adds. 'Maybe because I am the youngest, but everybody has been showing me what to do, giving me a lot of advice. They have been really nice.'

The cheeky Italian champ, whose favourite dance is the jive, is setting his sights on the final from day one.

'I think it is a big competition because there are a lot of good dancers, but I want to be in the final, definitely' he says. 'We will do our best.'

Craig Revel Horwood

He may have celebrated his 50th birthday since the last series but this year's batch of ballroom newbies should be warned: Craig Revel Horwood hasn't mellowed with age.

'I'm not going to give anyone an easy ride,' he promises. 'In fact, I'm going to get more critical. I was too soft last year, way too soft. I'm not going to be mean, just really honest, but people don't like that very much.'

Even so, Craig is looking forward to seeing the latest line-up strut their stuff.

'Overall it's a really good mix,' he says. 'There's a great cross section of people and the characters are quite strong. When you think of Jeremy Vine versus Peter Andre, they're chalk and cheese. And there are some real wild cards, like Ainsley Harriott. Anything could happen.'

How are you feeling ahead of this series?
I'm really excited. The celebrities are great. I like the idea that Ainsley is in there because he has a huge, fantastic personality, and he's a real practical joker. But it will be interesting to see if he can settle down in ballroom and keep a straight face. There are some fit young guys in there, with the likes of Anthony Ogogo and Peter Andre, and they're going to be going up against one another for the best Latin.

Who do you have your eye on for the final?
My eye is definitely on Anthony both because of his fitness level and his likeability. I think he is going to change the image of boxers on *Strictly*, because in the past they've been terrible. Georgia May Foote looks like a contender because of what she's done before at stage school, and I have high hopes for Kirsty Gallacher. She has a sports mentality that is perfect when it comes to criticism, because they tend to take it the right way and turn it into a positive.

Who will look good on the dance floor?
Anthony Ogogo and Georgia May Foote, who is simply gorgeous. We want to see both of them in all the Latin stuff, please. I think they're going to make husbands and wives happy at the same time.

Happy to see Claudia back for her second year?
Claudia did amazingly well last year. It's a difficult role to step up to and it's lovely having a female double act in Claudia and Tess. There aren't that many – French and Saunders, Mel and Sue – but this is our glamour version. Claudia is very funny, totally kooky and off the wall, and her timing is extraordinary.

What did you think of last year's finalists?
Last year was fantastic and I would have been happy with any of the finalists winning, but, it was great that it went to a bit of an underdog in Caroline Flack. She was extremely shocked about the whole thing.

What was your favourite moment of last year?
The stand-out dance was Jake Wood's salsa. It was just wonderful to see that coming from someone you least expect to be able to dance. The stand-out dance for all the wrong reasons was Scott Mills's crab dance. But he is funny. I love him on the radio. And that's exactly where he should stay!

Jeremy Vine

As a journalist, Jeremy knows how to put a spin on a story – but taking a spin on the dance floor is a different matter.

'I'm incredibly nervous,' he admits. 'Journalists don't do anything unprepared. If you're doing an interview you research it thoroughly and plan your questions. Now I'm going on a dance show and I can't dance. It's the other end of the spectrum.'

The BBC broadcaster, who will dance with Karen Clifton, was put in charge of the famous swingometer for the 2015 general election, but he's not sure his own moves will register high on the *Strictly* swing charts.

'John Sergeant was a colleague for years and I loved him on the show, but I decided I can't be the comedy dancer like him,' he says. 'So the only thing I can do is try and put one foot in front of the other and not fall over. You'll see a look of concentration on my face you've never seen before.'

At six foot three, Jeremy is one of the tallest of this year's contestants, a fact that he believes may count against him.

'I'm a Chelsea fan and the best player we ever had was Zola, who was very short. I once asked my mum why the best footballers are short and she said, "Their brain is closer to their feet." So I wonder if being tall is a disadvantage.

'In rehearsals, Natalie Lowe saw me struggling and she said, "Three words. Dance your height." If I learn nothing else, that will help me. It's not about dipping down to your partner, it's about being six foot three. If you are, live with it. At least you can run out of the studio fast when you're eliminated.'

The Radio 2 presenter has plenty of support from the sidelines, with wife Rachel and kids Martha, 11, and Anna, 8, cheering him on.

'My kids really love the show and they kept saying to me, "Why don't you go on *Strictly*?", so when I was asked I had nowhere to go on that one. They are just before the stage when they start to be hugely embarrassed by me, although they are already building a pile of sofas to hide behind.'

Jeremy, who turned 50 this May, does hide a secret musical past, as a drummer in a punk band called Flared Generation. But he's not convinced of his musicality.

'If you've heard punk music, there is no sense of rhythm among punk drummers,' he laughs. 'It's more like violence towards the nearest instrument. Unfortunately that doesn't help at all!'

Karen Clifton

Since they both reached the finals last year, Karen and fellow pro Kevin Clifton have tied the knot, hence the change of name from Hauer.

'It feels wonderful to be on the show as a married couple, especially as *Strictly* is such a family show,' says Karen. 'I am now officially a Clifton. I own everything that Kevin owns so if he ends up winning the glitterball it will feel like I won it.'

Earlier in the year, the happy couple choreographed the first dance for Karen's series 12 partner Mark Wright and bride Michelle Keegan, but they decided to wing it for their own nuptials.

'We danced the way we felt and we were really happy,' she reveals. 'We had a choir to sing for our first dance. They were a group of kids from very tough backgrounds that came together to sing, and for most of them it was their first time in London. To see them all smiling and having a great time at our wedding was beautiful.'

The Venezuelan-born dancer, who came fourth last year with *TOWIE* star Mark, is putting broadcaster Jeremy Vine through his paces this season and says 'he is the loveliest man ever'.

'What I love about him is that he's really intelligent, but there's a dark horse in there,' she says. 'He definitely wants to get down and boogie.'

Despite Jeremy's own admission that he dances like he's 'stuck in a lift', Karen thinks her new partner shows promise.

'The fact that he knows his left foot from his right foot is a good start,' she jokes. 'He walks in a straight line so I'm happy with that. I've yet to test him out but when I saw him doing a little solo, in the group routine, he seemed to stay on his timing and get the steps right so I think he'll be OK.

'A little bit of training and a little bit of discipline, and he'll be on the right path.'

Karen, whose other celeb partners include Nicky Byrne and Dave Myers, revealed Mark Wright was 'jealous' he wouldn't be dancing this year.

'I think he wants to do it all over again,' she laughs.

'I'm looking forward to my new partner but I also miss all of my previous partners. The three I've had so far have been completely different but hilarious in their own ways, and they're all good friends. I can't wait for Jeremy to join that list.'

Joanne Clifton

After making her debut on last year's *Strictly*, Joanne has danced her way into a new role as a resident expert on *It Takes Two*. So big brother Kevin is in for plenty of stick.

'I'm very excited because I'm making up the dance-expert panel with Karen Hardy, Ian Waite and Robin Windsor,' says Joanne. 'We'll be commenting on the couples so I just can't wait until it comes round to my brother! I'll obviously say his partner is great but Kevin is rubbish; he's the one letting her down.' she jokes.

Joanne, who remains part of the pro dancing team for the main show, made quite an impact dancing with DJ Scott Mills last year and provided some of the most memorable moments of the series.

'Scott tried hard, bless him, but he struggled a bit,' laughs Joanne. 'We went out on our best dance, the foxtrot to *The Addams Family* theme, and he danced it really well. Of course, he also did the crab dance to "Under the Sea" which appeared on all the programmes of the best moments of 2014, which was great.'

The Grimsby dancer also partnered astrologer and former *Strictly* star Russell Grant on the Christmas special, and she remains close to both.

'Scott and I got on really well and we still get together for a drink,' he said. 'Russell and I have sleepovers at his house, where we watch musicals and eat Chinese food. So I've made two really good friends.'

As an *ITT* expert, Joanne has her eye on one particular pop star in this year's competition, but she thinks anyone can win.

'Peter Andre will be great, especially with Janette,' she says. 'There will be fireworks going off when they dance, so I'm putting them in the final already. I think Jay is going to be really good; he's got a fantastic posture.

'But it's a hard one because normally you can guess who will go a long way and who will go out early, but this year, for different reasons, I think all of them are good. So whether it's because of their personality, their dance ability or their following, I couldn't call it.'

Joanne was recently bridesmaid at Kevin's wedding to fellow dancer Karen Hauer, and she jokes that the Cliftons are slowly taking over the show.

'My mum and dad were on it three years ago, in Blackpool, with their dance school, and I was an extra,' she says. 'If we bring the dog in next year the whole family will have been on.'

DICTIONARY OF DANCE

Don't know your Botafogo from your fleckerl? Can't tell a *gancho* from a gaucho? Have no fear, help is here. Swot up on our *Strictly* glossary and you'll soon be sounding as dance-y as Darcey. So next time the judges are giving someone a dressing-down for their dodgy ronde, you'll know exactly what they mean.

arch turn

Nothing to do with Craig's withering critique. It's a ballroom move where a woman turns right under her own raised right hand and/or a man turns left under his own raised left hand. The two arms form an arch.

armography

A term, apparently coined by Craig, meaning arm movements during any dance. Macmillan Dictionary online quotes the *SCD* judge in its definition: 'The armography was very blocky and wooden and showing absolutely no sign of expression whatsoever.'

Botafogo

Named after a beach resort in Rio de Janeiro, the Botafogo is a travelling walk with a change of direction from left to right or right to left and is used in the samba.

chainé

A continuous chain of turns in the same direction, in which one full turn is made with each two steps.

chassé

A turn consisting of three steps, where the feet are closed on the second or third step.

Cuban motion

Another name for that tricky hip action the judges love to see in the Latin dances. The hip rotation is caused by the alternate bending and straightening of the knees.

Cuban walks

Forward or backward walks with the aforementioned hip action thrown in.

cucaracha

Translating as 'cockroach', this is a basic salsa step, which breaks out to alternate sides, as follows:
Step 1: Take left foot out to side, transferring your full weight on to the left leg.
Step 2: Transfer weight back to the right foot.
Step 3: Close left foot to right foot. Repeat with right foot.

fleckerl

One of Len's favourites. A standing turn, often used in the Viennese waltz. Unlike the natural and reverse turns, the couple does not travel but rotates on the spot.

gancho

Literally meaning 'hook'. That cute little move in the Argentine tango, when one dancer hooks a leg around their partner's leg. Not to be confused with the hot, sweaty Argentinian cowboy coming back from the pampas that Len likes to talk about. He's a gaucho.

heel lead

A ballroom step where the heel of the leading leg makes the initial contact with the floor. The toe is lowered as the rest of the weight is placed on the leg.

heel turn

A turn on the heel of the supporting leg with the other foot held close and parallel. At the end of the turn the weight is transferred from one foot to another. The weight then transfers to the closing foot at the end of the turn.

kick-ball change

Nifty little move with a small kick of the lower leg, then a return to the ball of the foot on the same leg before shifting weight to the ball of the foot on the other leg.

musicality

One of Darcey's favourite words. The ability to hear and interpret music in an expressive and technically correct way.

natural turn

A turn to the right.

New Yorker

A four-beat step that starts with a couple facing each other, then 'opening' before repeating on the other side. Beat: 2, 3, 4 and 1.
• Start facing each other, with one hand held.
• Place your weight on the opposite leg from the joined hand and swivel to 'open' the partnership, stepping forward on the other leg, so that you are standing side by side, with your free arm extended.
• Swivel back to face your partner and join both hands.
• Repeat on the other side.

reverse turn

A turn to the left.

rise & fall

The use of the feet, ankles and legs to bring the body up and down during ballroom dances. Len is always on the lookout for this in the waltz.

ronde

Meaning 'round'. A pointed foot makes a circling action from front to back or vice versa.

samba roll

Rolling action performed by couples in hold, or in shadow hold, with the man behind the woman. The bodies roll in unison, from the waist up.

shimmy

A sexy little shake of the upper body achieved by alternating shoulder movements forward and backward. Much harder than it looks.

volta

Travelling step to the side, with one foot repeatedly crossing in front of the other, and a circular hip movement.

STAGE ENTERTAINMENT AND PHIL MCINTYRE ENTERTAINMENTS
IN ASSOCIATION WITH BBC WORLDWIDE PRESENT

BBC

Strictly Come Dancing

THE LIVE TOUR

FABULOUS

BOOK NOW!

2016 TOUR

22 – 24 Jan	**BIRMINGHAM** Barclaycard Arena	0844 338 8000	3 – 4 Feb	**NEWCASTLE** Metro Radio Arena	0844 493 666
26 – 27 Jan	**SHEFFIELD** Arena	0114 256 5656	5 – 7 Feb	**GLASGOW** The SSE Hydro	0844 395 400
28 – 29 Jan	**LEEDS** First Direct Arena	0844 248 1585	9 – 10 Feb	**NOTTINGHAM** Capital FM Arena	0843 373 300
30 – 31 Jan	**MANCHESTER** Arena	0844 847 8000	11 – 12 Feb	**LONDON** The SSE Arena, Wembley	0844 815 081.
2 Feb	**LIVERPOOL** Echo Arena	0844 8000 400	13 – 14 Feb	**LONDON** The O2	0844 8 24 48 2

 facebook.com/strictlylive

strictlycomedancinglive.com

@SCD_Live_Tour

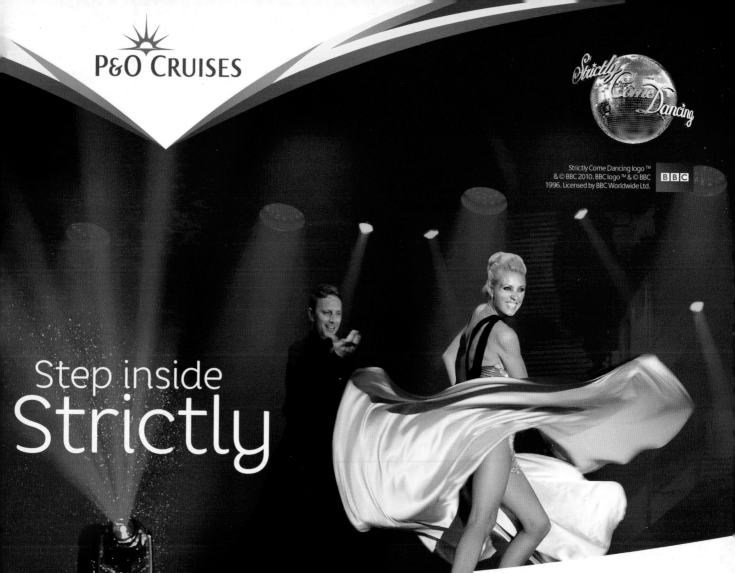

P&O CRUISES

Strictly Come Dancing

Step inside Strictly

Feel closer to the action than ever before on a P&O Cruises Strictly Come Dancing Themed Cruise.

We've officially teamed up with Britain's best-loved TV show to create the ultimate holiday for Strictly fans. Mingle with your favourite stars as you sail in complete comfort around the best of the Med or Canaries. Take in breathtaking destinations, Pasodobles, and Cha-Chas. Learn some moves and (if you've got the nerve) show them off for the judges.

So book today if you'd like to add some Strictly pizzazz to your next holiday.

This is the life

Canary Islands
22 APR - 6 MAY 2016 | 14 NIGHTS
Ventura N611

Southampton - Seville (tours from Cadiz)
Agadir - Lanzarote - Gran Canaria - La Palma
Madeira - Lisbon - Southampton

Canary Islands
16 MAY - 29 MAY 2016 | 13 NIGHTS
Britannia B614

Southampton - Madeira - La Palma
Gran Canaria - Lanzarote - Agadir
Lisbon - Southampton

Canary Islands
5 JUN - 18 JUN 2016 | 13 NIGHTS
Britannia B616

Southampton - Madeira - La Palma
Tenerife - Lanzarote - Lisbon - Vigo
Southampton

Mediterranean
22 JUL - 5 AUG 2016 | 14 NIGHTS
Azura A619

Southampton - Gibraltar - Ajaccio
Rome (tours from Civitavecchia)
Florence/Pisa (tours from La Spezia)
Monte Carlo - Marseilles - Seville (tours
from Cadiz) Southampton

Select Price Cruise
N611 From
£1,049pp†

POCRUISES.COM/STRICTLY-COME-DANCING
0843 373 0077 | VISIT A TRAVEL AGENT

Calls cost 5p per minute plus your telephone company's network access charge.

2 3 4 5 6 7 8 9 10

BBC Books, an imprint of Ebury Publishing
20 Vauxhall Bridge Road,
London SW1V 2SA

BBC Books is part of the Penguin Random House group of companies
whose addresses can be found at global.penguinrandomhouse.com

 Penguin
Random House
UK

Strictly Come Dancing Logo © BBC 2015, BBC logo © BBC 1996
Devised by the BBC and licensed by BBC Worldwide limited.
Text by Alison Maloney
Copyright: Woodland Books Ltd 2015
Images pp.30-37 by Guy Levy © Woodland Books Ltd.
Illustrations pp.86-91 © Grace Helmer
All other images © BBC

This book is published to accompany the television series
entitled *Strictly Come Dancing* first broadcast on BBC One in 2015.

Executive producer: Louise Rainbow
Series Director: Nikki Parsons
Series producers: Sarah James and Robin Lee Parrella

BBC Books would like to thank Jack Gledhill, Selena Harvey,
Tessa Beckett, Mike Griffith, Harriet Frost, Theresa Hewlett,
Vicky Gill and the Strictly Come Dancing Production team.

First published by BBC Books in 2015

www.eburypublishing.co.uk

A CIP catalogue record for this book is available from the
British Library

ISBN 9781849909945

Commissioning editor: Lorna Russell
Project editor: Grace Paul
Design: Karin Fremer

Printed and bound in Italy by Printer Trento SpA

Penguin Random House is committed to a sustainable future
for our business, our readers and our planet. This book is made
from Forest Stewardship Council ® certified paper.

 MIX
Paper from
responsible sources
FSC® C018179